The Art of Ritual

The Art of Ritual

A Guide To Creating and Performing Your Own Rituals for Growth and Change

Renee Beck and Sydney Barbara Metrick

CELESTIALARTS

Berkeley, California

CELESTIAL ARTS
P. O. Box 7327
Berkeley, California 94707

Cover design by Ken Scott
Cover art and interior illustrations by Terry Hatcher
Text design and production by David Charlsen
Composition by Recorder Typesetting Network

Library of Congress Cataloging-in-Publication Data
Beck, Renee, 1951–
     The art of ritual : a guide to creating and performing your own
  rituals for growth and change / Renee Beck and Sydney Barbara
  Metrick. — 1st ed.
        p.   cm.
     Bibliography: p.
     Includes index.
     ISBN 0-89087-582-0
     1. Rites and ceremonies.   2. Spiritual life.   I. Metrick, Sydney
  Barbara, 1947–   II. Title
  BL600.B43 1990
  291.3′8—dc20   89-33894
                                                                        CIP

First Printing, 1990

0 9 8 7 6 5 4 3
95 94 93 92

Manufactured in the United States of America

This book is dedicated to our parents:

Roie Beck,
who instilled in me a great wonderment
for ritual, God, and mystery

and

Sylvia and George Metrick,
who allowed me to become who I am.

Acknowledgments

We wish to thank Peter Beren for the opportunity to create this work, and for connecting us with the wonderful folks at Celestial Arts. We extend our deepest appreciation to David Charlsen for his skill and elegance in editing and design. We are also grateful to Tobey Kaplan for her astute editorial comments. Special thanks to Terry Hatcher, whose delightful artwork brings beauty to the pages of this book.

Renee extends great appreciation to the Holy One for making the process go so smoothly all down the line.

Contents

Foreword

All cultures recognize the need to ritualize major life transitions. In 1929, anthropologist Arnold Van Gennep coined the term "rite of passage" to describe the universal practice of ceremonializing life's major events, including: 1) birth—newness; 2) entry—making contact with others; 3) initiation—willingness to learn something new and be tested on it; 4) marriage/mergence—capacity for commitment, integration, and unifying opposites; 5) demonstration—ability to facilitate, heal, teach, guide; 6) attainment—inner contentment, modeling a skill or talent; and 7) death—letting go, moving out from the old into the new.

In his introduction to Van Gennep's *Rites of Passage* Solon Kimbala said that it is likely "'that one dimension of mental illness may arise because an increasing number of individuals are forced to accomplish their transitions alone and with private symbols." In *The Art of Ritual*, authors Beck and Metrick have created a practical healing manual that provides specific steps and guidelines for rituals. Their book will help individuals and groups to learn the art of supporting life changes as well as how to honor the space and time between transitions, an equally important subject largely ignored by this culture. Bill Bridges, in his book *Transitions: Making Sense of Life's Changes,* calls the area between changes "the neutral zone." The Africans refer to this as "walking the land of gray clouds." We might call this time "the land of I-don't know."

Our culture has not learned how to support the time between rites of passage, or how to honor the need to take the time to incorporate life experiences. During most major life events, for example, a person in this culture is supported strongly for a few weeks or a month, but after that support problems surface. A person between jobs might be asked, "Well, when are you going to get your next job?" A recently married couple might be asked, "When are you going to have a baby?" Someone experiencing the death of a loved one might be asked, "When are you going to get going again?" The minimum time required by an individual to integrate a consequential life experience is one year, and some people require two years. If one doesn't take time to absorb these experiences when they occur, they can emerge years later and cause other problems, such as untimely depression or unresolved grief. Our lives may be running smoothly, yet a sense of meaningless may be present. Such unhappy states indicate unresolved transitions surfacing.

One way this culture recognizes the need to ritualize and support change in others is by sending greeting cards. Our society, as it accelerates at a faster rhythm, experiences change at a swifter pace. Greeting cards are quick, efficient messages of support in our rapidly changing world. However, in a slower-moving society where spending time with an individual or family is a major way of extending support, greeting cards would not be appropriate.

To survive in the 21st Century, people must become more capable of handling change than ever before. Alvin Toffler elaborates on this idea in his visionary book *Future Shock,* when he states, ". . . We have the opportunity to introduce additional stability points and rituals into our society, such as new holidays, pageants, ceremonies, and games. Such mechanisms could not only provide a backdrop of continuity in everyday life but serve to integrate societies, and cushion them somewhat against the fragmenting impact of super-industrialism." Essentially, the challenge in the next century will be to become "the change master," a term Rosabeth Moss Kanter introduced in the 1980s. Kanter identifies ways we cope, manage, resist, or creatively approach change.

This book, *The Art of Ritual,* gives "Ten Guidelines for Creating Your Own Rituals" to assist you during times of change. Beck and Metrick also give examples of ways that you can integrate your experience. They remind us that human beings have used ritual for centuries as an important buffer to change, and as a way of consciously recognizing and supporting a life event rather than denying or indulging in it. *The Art of Ritual* provides a structure to recall the truth of Novalis' statement, "The seat of the soul is where the outer and inner worlds meet." Ritual provides the bridge between inner and outer worlds, and creates a context for reconnecting to the seat of our souls. The end result of all ritual is increased balance, strength, energy, and comfort. This is an important book whose time has come.

—Angeles Arrien
Cultural Anthropologist

Introduction

Transitions are often a form of crisis, an emotionally signifi-
cant event or radical change of status in a person's life; an
unstable or crucial time. In our secularized, technological-
ly sophisticated society, the existential isolation that all humans
experience is exacerbated during a crisis. In our desperate need to
find support, connection, or solace, we often focus an exaggerated
amount of energy on inappropriate people, substances, or pas-
times. As a recent *New York Times* article stated, "These days almost anyone might have an addiction. If it isn't to drugs or
alcohol, it's to food, cigarettes, exercise, relationships, sex, shopping, work, or even video games." These "addictions" offer an intimate connection or relationship which, although not fulfilling our
real needs, seems to offer some form of appeasement.

Unfortunately, during a crisis, these substitutes may de-power
rather than empower as we become increasingly more needy. The
inner confidence and power we seek has been culturally dis-
placed. In our society, the search for power has become a hall-
mark, and relentless striving for that power has become
instrumental in creating stress and breakdown on a grand scale.
The rituals followed in the acquisition of power can threaten both
life and humanity.

From teenagers seeking initiation into the adult world with
self-created rites involving dress, music, and language, to busi-
nesswomen establishing a new tradition in dress and language as
a support to identity, we see the attempt to engender timely and
appropriate rituals. Whether one is part of a minority because of
age, gender, race, religion, sexual orientation, or a handicap, and
whether membership in the minority group is permanent (as in
race or sex) or temporary (as in adolescence), there is an impera-
tive need for recognition and acceptance that welcomes and includes one's differences. Unfortunately, we are often made to feel
that unless we give up or hide that which makes us unique, we
have no place in society. The rituals our ancestors used to affirm
their identities or passages may be lost or outmoded.

We experience the crises in our lives no less deeply than our
ancestors did, yet we have few nurturing rituals to provide aid,
hope, and meaning in the passage through modern times. Accordingly, we have designed this book of ritual guidelines to offer you
the means to help yourself, and others, through life's transitions.
When you turn to this book to help you create a ritual to drama-
tize, comment on, and shape an event, you are giving yourself the
opportunity to be "at cause." You are empowering yourself.

There is a contemporary psychological concept called "locus
of control." The locus of control construct is a generalized expect-
ancy that one's outcomes are contingent more on one's own ef-

forts than on outside forces such as luck, fate, or the power of others. The former is said to characterize persons with an internal locus of control, whereas the latter characterizes individuals with an external locus of control. When people have an internal locus of control, they feel that by their acts they can have some control, and thus some power in their lives.

Rollo May in *Power and Innocence* states, "Power is the ability to cause or prevent change." He names five kinds of power: "**Exploitative**—subjects the weak to the strong with no concern for the needs of the weak. **Manipulative** is power over another that requires the collusion, collaboration, and cooperation of the weaker. **Competitive** power is used against another person. **Nutrient** power is used to meet the needs of the other. **Integrative** power is used with another to build a better life for both. Synergistics is another way of stating it. Power is made available to the community and everyone's power is shared."[1]

This book is designed to provide empowerment through nutrient and integrative power. Bringing rituals into your life will empower you. Rituals will allow you to have more choices, to gain perspective on changes. Rituals offer you tradition, support, and an increased grasp of relatedness, as well as a greater sense of balance to help you improve your life.

As rituals become a part of your life, you may find they enrich even simple things. When you are performing the ritualized behaviors of preparing for a presentation at a meeting, planning a slumber party for your children, or making a brunch for your friends, you will have a new awareness. Perceiving these everyday acts as having the potential to contain the sacred makes them more special and lets you contribute to them your own unique gifts.

It is our belief that through knowledge and understanding of ritual we can gain access to timeless wisdom and attain the sense that being is of value in and of itself. To that end, we are presenting the basic elements and processes common to all rituals in an attempt to provide an understanding of how rituals work, as well as the knowledge necessary to create rituals for various occasions. The principles involved are simple but effective. We hope to help you understand the rituals you already use, bring new meaning and depth to ritualized events such as birthdays, New Year's Eve, and housewarmings, and develop new rituals where they might be needed in your lives. Beyond this, we hope that the integration of the principles presented here will lend a structure to your consciousness that increases the meaning in your day-to-day life. While ritual is a tool to bridge the gap between the sacred and the mundane, we believe that "ordinary" life is sacred, as the expression of Spirit.

---

1. Rollo May, *Power and Innocence* (New York: W.W. Norton and Co., 1972), pp. 105ff.

Chapter 1

How To Use This Book

We would like to share some ideas and techniques that have been a source of support, honor, and assistance through various life transitions. We have found that using personal rituals has been important in our individual lives, as it has been for our friends, students, and clients. Hopefully, you will find this book a reference to inspire and benefit you.

The chapters in this book are a step-by-step guide to learning and utilizing the concepts fundamental to practicing ritual. Each chapter blends with the others to form a seamless whole. As you read and absorb one chapter, your ability to understand and use the subsequent one will improve. Therefore, we recommend that you read each section before attempting to design your own rituals, even if the ideas in a specific chapter seem intriguing enough to make you want to start right in.

If you are new to the world of ritual, this is especially important. If you happen to be experienced in the practice of ritual, it may still be valuable to familiarize yourself with the particular concepts and processes we discuss, so that you can blend your style with the approach presented here.

Any ritual you design will be an attempt to return to a sense of wholeness that has been altered by transition. Whether the rite is to be an effort to correct an imbalance or celebratory of positive change, the growth that results from the planning, preparation, and manifestation should be a reflection of the wholeness contained in the ritual itself.

Take your time. Acquaint yourself with the types of rituals that are discussed in Chapter 4. As you become familiar with the categories, you may begin realizing how different parts of your life fall into one or another grouping. Think about how you currently address or neglect these transitions, and make a mental note regarding those passages in your life where you might consider introducing ritual.

Chapter 5 introduces the process for creating and performing a ritual. The concept of process can be difficult for "Western minds" to accept. Process is not just an approach or method, but a practice. The values of our society have oriented us toward goals, achievements, and results. The letters ASAP form a familiar command: As Soon As Possible! Yet the importance of the journey, weighed against arrival at the destination, is interesting to consider. It is the journey that gives the destination worth.

Familiarizing yourself with the developmental stages that unfold during a process, and cultivating the careful attention and patience a process requires, will help you create rituals with increased power and meaning. Even more important, as you develop the concept of process, your normal life can lose some of the stressful urgency that each of us experiences.

We all have different tools that help us cope. Our techniques vary in their efficacy. When we are in demanding situations it is not uncommon to rely on some resources past their point of usefulness. You may be a runner, a coffee drinker, or a smoker. Perhaps you bake bread, shoot baskets, or listen to music when you need to come back to yourself. Each of these things works for a reason, as you will see in Chapter 6 where we introduce you to the Elements. These are capitalized throughout the book to help you recognize them as symbols of archetypal qualities. The information in this section can help you identify the ways you lose your equilibrium during changes. Baking bread may ground you or get you in touch with the Element of Earth. Smoking may seem to clear your head and give you greater access to the Element of Air. By working with the Element Selection Guide, you can bring more resources to your daily life as you learn to choose Elemental symbols for ritual harmony.

Finding a way to make these symbols tangible turns them from concepts to useful tools. In Chapter 7, there are simple instructions for making tools that serve as power objects. Bringing these power objects into your rituals is one way a ceremony becomes a sacred rite. The way your tools are used as part of the ritual creates another opportunity to transform the energy of the ceremony into a moving and magical experience.

Chapter 8 contains information on setting up altars. An altar is a kind of mirror with each of the Elements symbolically represented in the balanced way you hope to become within yourself. As you arrange your altar, you can reflect on the connection with your inner state.

There are basic principles involved in the design and use of altars. As you become familiar with the principles, you will be able to recognize the expression of the sacred in even the simplest altar. An altar is a place from which you work, the place that holds your ritual tools and power objects. Setting up an altar that holds these objects in a sacred and balanced way is the first step toward creating the same balance within.

When you reach Chapter 9, Ritual Guidelines and Worksheet, you will be comfortable with all of the aspects and details of creating a successful ritual. Here you will be aided by the step-by-step worksheet where you will find a number of actual ceremonies that have been designed to describe each of the ritual types we have categorized: beginnings, mergings, cycles, endings, and healings. These samples have been subcategorized in two specific ways. (1) In each of the five categories there will be a sample designed for individual use, one for two individuals in a relationship, one for a family, and one for a group. (2) In each of those subcategories, you will find a ritual example for the physical world of manifestation, the feeling world of deepening, the mental world of relatedness, and the spiritual world of initiation. Some of the rituals described will be directly useful, and if not, adaptable to your needs.

In Chap. 11 we have presented two complete rituals that follow each step as shown in Chapter 5. Here, you will be able to find insight and ideas you can bring to your own rituals.

Chapter 12 contains a table of Elemental correspondences, and a summary to help you integrate the knowledge you have gained.

There is an art to the creation of a successful ritual. Each ceremony is a dramatic event that opens the door to another world. Entering this world is similar to what you might experience during a movie, play, concert, or religious service. You can become so absorbed in the experience that the feelings evoked remove you from where, and even who, you are. The world you enter through ritual is a timeless one. It lies within you, in a place often unremembered, and around you, in a place often beyond reach.

Chapter 2

Understanding The Role of Ritual in Your Life

A ritual, a rite, a ceremony, a series of symbolic acts focused toward fulfilling a particular intention. We often think of ritual as belonging to the realm of religion, but in fact, rituals are an integral part of nature and of our daily lives. Animals have ritualized ways of defining and defending their territory. Humans do, as well. Animals and birds often have elaborate courting and mating rituals, again, not unlike humans. Finding, collecting, preparing, and eating food is another behavior that is ritualized for us as it is in nature. When you look at survival or social behavior, you generally will see ritual.

What we intend to focus on in this book are not the unconscious rituals that give form to life, but the ones that are consciously created with intentionality. There are many unconscious rituals in our daily lives: the morning coffee and newspaper, tucking the children into bed with a story, playing softball with your friends every week, or sleeping in on Sunday mornings. Other rituals that have a place in your life, that have a more conscious intent and sense of magic, fall into the category of holidays. These are occasions like birthdays, weddings, winter celebrations, graduation ceremonies, and baby showers. Certainly the celebration of these events can offer a sense of enhanced meaning, an opportunity for increased social connection, and a deepening of tradition. What the *traditional rituals* may not provide is something that speaks to your individual needs in a profound and meaningful manner.

The Purpose of Ritual

Transitions or turning points, even when positive, signify moving toward something new and possibly unfamiliar. What *was* may be

"The essence of ritual is that something done in the physical realm is related to the higher worlds. This may be a simple gesture of the hand or an elaborate ceremony. It can be working consciously in everyday life, so that quite mundane actions become full of meaning, or a carefully designed ritual acted out for a specific occasion ... Ritual is the mode of formalizing action and giving it not only meaning, but creating a contact with other worlds."

—*Halevi*
School of Kabbalah

incorporated and used as a springboard toward the new, or it may be left behind. Those aspects of change—the unknown ahead, and the loss of what was—can make the experience of change difficult. We often undergo a period of feeling out of balance until we can accustom ourselves to the differences. Even when the life change is a sought-after improvement like a new job, it is not uncommon to find that the first weeks bring the confusion and insecurity of adjusting to a new role, new co-workers in a new environment, and new responsibilities. These adjustments can supersede the pride and elation that initially accompanied the job move. Discovering ways to incorporate and adjust to the newness can be a demanding challenge. It entails finding an equilibrium between the outer expression of the change and our inner relationship to it. Possible ways of accomplishing this at the new workplace may include improving and deepening communication with co-workers, clearly defining your job responsibilites, and getting support from friends and family during this time of adjustment. When this inner-outer balance occurs, we may realize a calming sense of wholeness.

On a transpersonal level, this wholeness is really never lost, but on a personal level, we can easily lose touch with it.

Bill Moyers, in conversation with Joseph Campbell, says, "The wise people of all times have said that we can live the good life if we learn to live spiritually ... How do we learn to live spiritually?" And Campbell replies, "In ancient times ... that was what ritual was for. A ritual can be defined as an *enactment* of a myth. By participating in a ritual, you are actually experiencing a mythological life. And it's out of that participation that one can learn to live spiritually."[2]

"People ... create images of themselves in the world and guide their action according to such images. The images are not only myths that capture the meaning of past experiences but lead to anticipation of future events."

—*N. Fredman and R. Sherwood*
Handbook of Structured Techniques in Marriage and Family Therapy

This is the purpose of creative ritual—increasing balance and connection within ourselves, with each other, the world, and with the larger rhythms and energies that bring stability and light to our lives. Many of the rituals that are available to us may seem empty. Our needs, as individuals and as a people, have changed. The traditional rituals may not meet or even recognize our current needs. When rituals are so finely woven into the fabric of our common expressions that we barely recognize them for what they are, much less tap into their inherent power, it is time to take a look at how we can actively bring ritual to a meaningful and relevant position once again. This requires first taking an honest look at our lives and the trends and values of our culture.

Once we are in touch with our identity we can create rituals appropriate to our needs. Our personal and cultural myths may unconsciously guide us, but offer little emotional support unless we can consciously express what they symbolize. Joseph Campbell sees mythology as having four functions. (1) **Mystical or metaphysical:** Its purpose is to bring the individual to a state of wonder at the mystery of it all—from the universal level to the personal level. (2) **Cosmological:** The function here is to bring the mystery, expressed in universal themes and motifs, to the people of each culture in a way that helps them understand their world. (3) **Sociological:** It provides a way of verifying, nurturing, and preserving the beliefs and customs of a culture or social order. (4) **Psychological:** Myth is a guide and a support to individuals from birth to death and through the difficult passages of human life. As we develop the ability to step back from life and see the stories we tell both individually and in the various groups to which we belong, we will then be looking at our myths; we can then use ritual to enact them in a way that empowers us.

The Relevance of Ritual

To derive the power from a ritual it must, in some way, stand apart from our ordinary lives. It is not uncommon for us to have so much of our energy and attention directed toward our daily routines and our goals that our focus becomes narrowed. We may even become preoccupied with our doubts, our fears, or our pain. These things can isolate us. We may lose connection with the rhythm in our lives and the passages that we all share as human beings on the planet. This is what the existential philosopher Martin Heidegger called a state of "forgetfulness of being."

On the other hand, there is the state of "mindfulness of being." This is a condition of authenticity, of being fully self-aware and conscious of being the creative composer of one's own life. Ritual provides us with a way of taking responsibility for our lives through the use of a metaphoric process. At the time of a milestone or rite of passage, we can shift our focus from the minutiae of the event to the way the experience fits into the grand plan of our life. The creativity, drama, and perceptual shift connected with the ritual enable us to dis-identify with the isolation, confusion, or fear that may be associated with the passage and to know instead the power of creativity, action, and understanding.

Ritual is often recognized as an art form. The ceremoniously performed acts of a ritual allow us to form a connection with the unconscious as we begin to speak its language. Not only can we access our individual unconscious, which holds that which has

"In fairytales, the movement toward wholeness—often symbolized by a quest for prince, princess or treasure—is constellated by the lack of something in the kingdom. Similarly, in any human society a new archetypal pattern will be constellated in the collective unconscious to compensate for what is missing in the consciousness of the collective."

—Marion Woodman
Addiction to Perfection

passed from awareness, but energy is summoned from the collective unconscious as well. Here we pass through our roots into our ancestral heritage, which is common to the human family. This essential energy is expressed as mythological motifs that transcend history and cultural differences, and establishes instead a fundamental sense of unity.

The Power of Ritual

"Directed energy causes change. To have integrity, we must recognize that our choices bring about consequences, and that we cannot escape responsibility for the consequences, not because they are imposed by some external authority, but because they are inherent in the choices themselves."

—Starhawk
Dreaming the Dark

A well designed and executed ritual is more than just a dramatic presentation. Through ritual we can enter a state of timelessness, which is sometimes called an altered state of consciousness. In this state, we can go beyond the parameters that have described our perception of reality. The transformative power of a ritual comes by way of this altered state, which Milton Erickson describes as a trance state.

> This healing or therapeutic condition of trance "is a period during which the limitations of one's usual frames of reference and beliefs are temporarily altered so one can be receptive to other patterns of association and modes of mental functioning that are conducive to problem solving."[3]

Erickson has developed a five-step paradigm for achieving therapeutic trance, which is parallel to what occurs in achieving any altered state. The steps are as follows:

> (1) fixation of attention, anything that fascinates and holds or absorbs a person's attention; (2) depotentiating habitual frameworks and belief systems, where the beliefs are more or less interrupted and suspended for a moment or two, during which time latent patterns of association and sensory-perceptual experience have an opportunity to assert themselves; (3 and 4) unconscious search and unconscious process, where a new experience or solution to a problem is sought and a creative moment can occur; and (5) the hypnotic response, an expression of behavioral potentials that are experienced as taking place autonomously."[4]

This timeless state, coupled with the expressive, moving, and even spectacular qualities of a dramatic ceremony, brings us to a grander level of experience—a level at which we can feel our own majesty.

When we use ritual to assist us through change, we gain authority not only from the enactment of the ritual but also from the intentional planning process. When the transition that initially brings the call for support is a difficult passage, it is not uncommon to feel diminished by the power of the change. With the loss of a spouse, we not only have to deal with mourning our loss, but we need to look ahead to a drastically different future. Even when change is something we seek, it is not always easy to accept. A teenager graduating from high school may feel proud of the accomplishment and excited to be free from the school system, but terrified about entering the "adult" world of work or higher education. Entering into the new situation means entering into something unfamiliar, into an arena where we have less control simply because of the unfamiliarity.

There is a resistance to change in the psychological world as well as the world of physics. Newton's first law states that an object will persist in its state of rest or uniform motion unless it is *compelled* to change. Unfortunately, or fortunately, we are often compelled to change. As long as we feel we have some sort of control over what is happening, we do not feel stripped of power. As we plan and prepare for the ritual event, we are involved in the process of *doing* versus *being done to*. This in itself is empowering.

We are all familiar with the difference in feeling between the empowerment of action and the powerlessness that can follow being acted upon. This is apparent even in the informal rituals that we enact to gain a sense of control over our lives. These are actions like fighting an unfair parking violation and leaving the courtroom fine-free and gratified. Although in a case like this we are still at the mercy of the machinations of "the system," we find there is opportunity, through our own creative response, to be more than a powerless victim. The same creativity that brings this option is the foundation of ritual expression. And the kind of power to which one is restored through the use of ritual is nothing less than a return to your own spiritual center, the home of your self-esteem.

"Any affect or emotion which in its raw and unaltered form is too intense to be controlled by will alone may need its ritual. Without ritual, such energies may inundate the ego and force it into acting out or into obsessive behavior. Ritual brings about containment and acceptance, control of intensity, and 'dosage.'"
—Edward Whitmont
Return of the Goddess

The Need for Ritual

As Western civilization has advanced, secularization has increased, and the connection to the sacred has declined. The individualism nourished by the "me generation" in the sixties opened us up to more acceptance of differences. Yet the diversity born from fearlessly seeking our differences distanced us from the spiritual containers previously provided by simple reliance on family, neighborhood, or church. We often found ourselves left on our own to deal with the changes in our lives. Solon T. Kimbala, in his introduction to Arnold van Gennep's *The Rites of Passage,* writes that it is likely "that one dimension of mental illness may arise because an increasing number of individuals are forced to accomplish their transitions alone and with private symbols."[5] As individuals, we need more relatedness, and better ways to find a balance within ourselves.

Socially, we need to create more balance as well. There is no denying that as a people and as a planet, we are in need of healing. Unless we find ways to achieve harmony within ourselves and in our relationships with others, and learn to consciously unite as members of a global family, the dangers we face will continue to increase. Mystical traditions propose that the one goal of personal growth is to become more conscious of all our relationships, inner and outer, and with our sense of Spirit, until we recognize it as a sense of unity or oneness among all things. Even if you are not spiritually inclined, the need for an increased awareness and balanced unification seems evident if we are to succeed in avoiding destruction of our species and our planet.

Ritual is one way to help this process of growth. People not presently involved with a traditional religion deserve access to safe and life-affirming ritual methods with which they can feel comfortable. Those within religious or spiritual traditions can benefit by a more conscious understanding of the rituals they utilize. Both can benefit by bringing awareness and intention to the secular rituals that are a regular part of life.

"Rituals are an expression of the human need to belong, to be part of a group."
—Fritz Perls
The Gestalt Approach and Eye Witness to Therapy

---

2. Joseph Campbell, *The Power of Myth* (New York: Doubleday, 1988), p. 182.

3. Milton Erickson and Ernest Rossi, *An Exploratory Casebook* (New York: Irvington Publishers, Inc., 1979), pp. 4-7.

4. Ibid., pp. 10-11.

5. Arnold van Gennep, *The Rites of Passage* (University of Chicago Press, Chicago, 1960), pp. xvii-xviii.

Chapter 3

Myth, History, and Symbol

Myth and History

The use of ritual is parallel with the emergence of humankind. Two to three million years ago, humans depended primarily on the hunt, and the first rituals were created to appease nature and ensure survival. Sacrifices were made to the hunted animals to guarantee that the tribes' needs for food would be met. These animals, such as the cave bear and the cave lion, were also seen to have a religious power and significance that led them to be used as totems. Such totems were used chiefly for protection, but were also seen as ways to provide an alliance with the animal pack.

There is evidence that 150,000 years ago Homosapiens neanderthalensis—the Neanderthal—dealt with the mystery of life by the ritual burial of their dead. Remains have been unearthed in Europe that held tools, weapons, and other objects that point to a belief in some sort of afterlife. Shrines were also found with altars to the animals slain in the hunts. These Paleolithic people were known for elaborate paintings depicting the hunt and the part the sorcerer or shaman played in it. The wondrous paintings of these hunters have been found in labyrinthine caves in France, and also in North Africa.

The totemistic hunters described above belonged to one of three basic types of primitive societies distinguished by Father W. Schmidt in *The Origin of the Idea of God.*

These groups with secret initiation rites, elaborate clan systems, and tribal traditions emphasize the role and authority of men, both in the religious and in the political organization of the symbolically articulated community. Another type of

"Since rituals make use of the same stuff that dreams are made of—symbolism, fantasy, myths, and metaphors, they address themselves to the most primitive and profound level of experience."
—Onno van der Hart
Rituals in Psychotherapy

peoples were involved with hunting, fishing and gathering. There was an essential equality between the sexes, with different tasks not promoting any special privileges or peculiar rights to command. A third type of people with a social organization almost completely antithetical to that of the hunting tribes could be found in the tropical gardening cultures. Here it was the women who enjoyed the magico-religious and social advantage. They were the bearers of children and chief producers of food[6]

The women of the Stone Age, in addition to being depicted in the many cave paintings, were also represented by carved female figures, often known as Venus figures. The small nude figures, with exaggerated breasts, bellies, and hips, are believed to embody the concept of fertility. Representing the archetypal female, they symbolize both the mystery of life and birth in women, as expressed by "Mother Earth." The people of the Stone Age were nature worshipers: The sunrise heralding the day, the sunset bringing on the night, the phases of the moon, and the passing of seasons were all mysteries that profoundly influenced their lives. Rituals were created to ensure the rising of the sun, the falling of the rain, and the fertility of the earth. We find the roots of many of our present celebrations in the rituals and holidays developed by these nature-worshiping peoples.

The primitive people of these early tribes used symbol and ritual in an instinctive way.

> Magic was the primordial form of human thought; it consisted in either spatiotemporal connection ("sympathetic magic," as when drinking the blood of an ox transfers its strength to the drinker) or phenomenal similarity ("imitative magic," as when the sound of drumming induces thunderheads to form). . .[7]

In a symbolic manner, a level of reality was ritually created that became the consensual reality of daily life.

Ancient history shows that the participation mystique of the earliest peoples was the directing force that created the numinous quality of their symbolic and real lives. This same quality of merging the subjective and objective belongs to all of us in our early years of childhood. The development of consciousness, in the individual as in the race, shifts the ways in which symbol and ritual are used; but perhaps the innate quality of magical thinking is what allows symbol, ritual, myth, and religion to manifest in our lives.

Symbols and the Collective Unconscious

Symbols have a level of universal meaning and a level of personal meaning. Symbols are the language of the unconscious mind, and according to Jungian psychology there is a personal unconscious (those memories from one's own history that are not immediately or easily available), as well as a collective unconscious.

> The collective unconscious may be thought of as an impersonal or transpersonal unconscious because as Jung says, "It is detached from anything personal and is entirely universal, and because its contents can be found everywhere, which is naturally not the case with personal contents." The collective unconscious is better conceived as an extension of the personal unconscious to its wider and broader base, encompassing contents which are held in common by the family, by the social group, by tribe and nation, by race, and eventually by all humanity. Each succeeding level of the unconscious may be thought of as going deeper and becoming more collective in its nature. The wonder of the collective unconscious is that it's all there, all the legend and history of the human race, with its unexorcised demons and its gentle saints, its mysteries and its wisdom, all within each one of us—a microcosm within the macrocosm. . .[8]

We can gain a better understanding of how symbols express the archetypal energies of the collective unconscious by exploring one of these archetypes. The archetypal feminine, exemplified by the earth mother figures described earlier, is one of these energies. This psychic phenomenon has been symbolically and ritually expressed from the magical phase of Paleolithic consciousness, through the mythological phase of Neolithic consciousness, into the Bronze and Iron Ages and beyond. We find this energy in the myths, rituals, and symbols of all times and cultures. In early times, the earth mother was known as the Mother Goddess or the Great Goddess. The Goddess energy represented not only creation and fertility but also death and a subsequent rebirth that began the cycle anew. This and other archetypal energies find their way into mythological motifs that support the universal nature of the collective unconscious. The death-rebirth cycle associated with the Great Goddess is itself an archetypal expression. The cycle of the opposites embraced within a whole, the dynamic interplay between these polar forces, and even more primarily, the undifferentiated state that precedes bifurcation, is recognized in other cultures with different symbols.

"In times past man's religion provided the link with the world of the unconscious. The inner realm of man was taken into account by man's religious outlook, and his mythology and cosmology were like charts of the soul. Once man lost this dimension to his religion he also lost contact with the unconscious. Rejected and separated from consciousness, the unconscious turned hostile and in our century has erupted in barbaric wars, crime, and the sickness of soul so characteristic of our times."
—John A. Sanford
Healing and Wholeness

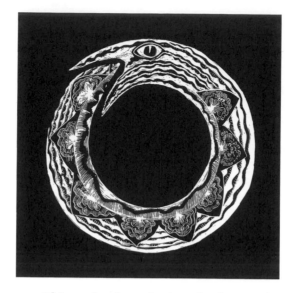

This cycle of continuity, also known as the Great Round, was symbolically depicted as the Ouroboros—the snake biting its own tail. The image of a snake is recognized as a powerful symbol universally. Among the meanings: transformation (the snake shedding its skin and being regenerated); creativity (the dynamic expansion represented by its phallic shape); temptation (the seduction of strength by matter); and inner strength (as in the yoga concept of kundalini energy). On the collective level, the meanings for the snake are many and often paradoxical. On a personal level, the associations one has with snakes may come from other sources. This could be the subjective interpretation one makes of the snake story in Genesis. Associations may come from a highly charged experience in one's personal history—having a family member with a snake phobia, for example. The connections that can be evoked are limitless.

The Function of Symbols

A symbol is something that represents something else. The role of symbols in ritual is largely as vehicles through which one can join forces with the essential concordance of the group, nature, the universe, or Spirit. Through the language of the unconscious, we address the deeper levels of our individual and collective selves when we use symbols. Paul Tillich, in *Theology and Symbolism*, wrote that this is the great function of symbols: to point beyond themselves with a power greater than the symbols themselves, "to open up levels of reality which otherwise are closed, and to open up levels of the human mind of which we otherwise are not aware."[9] If you were to study mythology, folklore, or comparative religion, it would soon become evident that many symbols and themes are repeated, sometimes only slightly altered, from culture to culture over time. The Christian sacrament of communion, or "eating the god" to make him a part of you, has parallels in many other traditions. In agrarian cultures, there is a ceremony performed at every harvest to insure the crop's abundance in the following year. This entails making a bread with the last sheaves of corn, and ritually consuming it. The ceremony is based on the belief that the "corn god" that lives in the crops will remain immortal as his life is transmuted. Similar rituals can be found in the traditions of pre-Columbian Aztecs, North American Creek Indians, and other peoples from India to Africa to Japan.

When one performs the symbolic act of eating (taking in, becoming one with, being nourished by) the fruit or bread that represents God or Spirit, the opportunity is afforded to experience something that could not otherwise be experienced. The symbol and the symbolic act that imply something greater provide the means to know or to be something greater than oneself—to move from the secular toward the sacred.

Symbols

Some symbols have a solely personal meaning. You may have symbolic objects in your life that hold meaning only for you. The back corner of your closet may hold a cherished pair of tattered old sneakers that you just can't throw away. You were wearing them when you scored the winning points in a basketball game. If anyone saw them they might think the pride associated with that occasion is the reason for your attachment to the sneakers. But for you they may symbolize something even greater—a turning point in your life. Others may not be aware of the insecurities you conquered to play in that game, or that you had to let go of the thought of possible humiliation in order to put every ounce of courage and effort into that critical shot—and you did it! Since that day you have walked in a different world, one in which you are more confident and courageous. The sneakers became a personal symbol of transformation for you.

Other symbols, although personal, may be shared. These are found frequently in relationships and families. One of our clients shared a family story that exemplifies this. When Cindy was seven, her mother, who loathed sewing, hand-stitched a family flag. She sewed a maroon symbol representing each family member onto a turquoise field. The household was quite proud of this flag and flew it in front of their home on family occasions and holidays. The flag became a symbol of unity for the family. Years later, after all the children had grown, left home, and started their own families, Cindy was one day honored by the gift of this flag. It became a treasured keepsake for her.

Mementos too, or souvenirs, often serve as symbols, not only to remind people of an experience they had but to bring forth the feelings that were associated with that time.

Just as families may have symbols that bring them a sense of unity, so do social groups, organizations, and even nations. These symbols bring a sense of tradition that binds the group in certain ways. The symbols may say something about the social relationships within the group, such as with uniforms and insignia, or they may express opinions and values common to the group. A logo including a dove or an olive branch, which are symbols for peace, is an example of this. Folklore and cultural myths are made of the symbols and motifs that prescribe the rituals of the group. As Joseph Campbell stated:

> These bits of information from ancient times, which have to do with the themes that have supported human life, built civilizations, and informed religions over millennia, have to do with deep inner problems, inner mysteries, inner thresholds of passage . . . . Once this subject catches you, there is such a feeling, from one or another of these traditions, of information of a deep, rich, life-vivifying sort that you don't want to give up.[10]

Funk and Wagnall's elaborates on this:

> The "group characteristics" which result from the accumulated nature of folklore [or myth, or ritual], and by which we attempt to recognize and label it, are not to be thought of as opposed to individuality. Folklore is something which the individual has in common with his fellows, just as all have eyes and hands and speech. It is not contrary to himself as an individual but a part of his equipment. It makes possible—perhaps it might be defined as that which constitutes—his rapport with his particular segment of mankind.[11]

When you are determining the symbols to use in a ritual, you are not only choosing things and acts that have a personal meaning for you, but perhaps unknown to you, the choices you make are likely to be tapping into a greater and more profound history that is accessible through your own unconscious. When we think of history, we generally think in a linear fashion of history being behind us. By considering history as being created cyclically, season after season, year after year, it may be easier to imagine it as the core somewhere within the unconscious.

Sacred Symbols

Symbols are an approach to the sacred as they represent common ideas and feelings from the whole of human existence, and fundamental concepts about all of existence. Eliade, in *The Two and the One,* states that:

> The man who understands a symbol not only "opens himself" to the objective world, but at the same time succeeds in emerging from his personal situation and reaching a comprehension of the universal . . . Thanks to the symbol, the individual experience is "awoken" and translated into a spiritual act. To "live" a symbol and correctly decipher its message implies an opening towards the Spirit and finally access to the universal.[12]

Symbols and ritual put us in touch with meaning and mystery in a way nothing else can. In "The Search for Signs of Intelligent Life in the Universe," Trudy the Bag Lady (played by Lily Tomlin) is pondering the meaning of life and says, ". . . the mystery of life. The operative word here is what? Mystery! Not meaning . . . Because at the moment you are most in awe of all there is about life that you don't understand, you are closer to understanding it all than at any other time."[13] That power that instills in us wonder and fear, although often incomprehensible or at least ineffable, is still compelling. We constantly seek to be moved beyond ourselves through music, art, dance, drama, nature, and love, as well as through participation in religious or spiritual activities. From teenagers at a rock concert to families gathered to hear Handel's "Messiah" at Christmas, the common experience produced by the music as well as the event is to be touched and expanded, to be able to turn to someone near you and see that the same feelings were evoked in them, and to feel that unity.

The power of these symbols not only moves us but instructs us. Sacred symbols, as the components of mythologies, form the underpinnings of each culture. In every culture the archetypes (basic energy patterns within the psyche) are represented in this way. Consider, for example, the gods and goddesses of ancient Rome: Juno, the jealous wife; Venus, goddess of love and beauty;

"Symbolism is organized in its vast, explanatory and creative function as a system of highly complex relations, one in which the dominant factor is always a polarity linking the physical and metaphysical worlds."

—*J. E. Cirlot*
A Dictionary of Symbols

Mars, the aggressive god of war; or Pluto, lord of Hades, domain of death and riches. These and many others were worshiped as deities, and at the same time they derived their power from the fact that they were reflections of the parts within each of us. Their battles are our battles, and their wisdom, ours as well.

6. Josepth Campbell, *Primitive Mythology* (New York: Penguin Books, 1987), pp 319-320.

7. Clifford Geertz, *Magic, Witchcraft, and Religion* (Palo Alto: Mayfield Publishing Co., 1985), p. 8.

8. June Singer, *Boundaries of the Soul* (New York: Anchor Press, 1973), p. 95.

9. Paul Tillich, "Theology and Symbolism" in *Religious Symbolism* (F. Ernest Johnson, New York, 1955), pp. 107-16, p. 109.

10. Joseph Campbell, *The Power of Myth* (New York: Doubleday, 1988), p. 4.

11. Funk and Wagnall, *Folklore, Mythology, and Legend* (San Francisco: Harper and Row, 1984), p. 400.

12. Mircea Eliade, *The Two and the One* (Chicago: University of Chicago Press, 1962), p. 201.

13. Jane Wagner, *The Search for Signs of Intelligent Life in the Universe* (New York: Harper & Row, 1986), p. 206.

Chapter 4

Types of Rituals

All rituals center around transition—changes that have happened, are happening, or may happen. These changes may be divided into five categories—beginnings, mergings, cycles, endings, and healings. Each of these touches on the archetypes you will find repeated a number of times in this book, and explained in detail in Chapter 6, The Elements of Ritual. These are: initiation or origin (the Element Fire), relatedness (Air), movement or deepening (Water), manifestation or completion (Earth), and wholeness or unity (Essence). Each category has its own integrity but simultaneously entails elements of some or all of the other categories. For example, marriage is a typical example of the merging rituals. Although the main theme of marriage is the coming together of two people to create a shared life, no less important is the ending of single life. This ending is casually addressed in rituals like bachelor parties. The newly married couple may begin life in a new dwelling, incorporating the category of beginnings. Marriage also necessitates the harmonizing of two individuals with different backgrounds, habits, and ways of being. Sometimes working out these differences requires that the couple enter therapy for each to resolve old individual wounds. Either of these would be a type of healing ritual. The merging, which results in a union greater than the two individuals, may itself provide access to healing. As the years pass and the couple grows together, they celebrate anniversaries, which are cyclical rituals.

Thus, what seems like one event can include the five facets covered by the ritual categories: beginnings, mergings, cycles, endings, and healings. Let us introduce you to the five categories, give you a few sample rituals, and begin to acquaint you with the suggested format, which is discussed in greater detail in the next chapter, The Process of Ritual.

Beginnings

"It's a girl!" states the banner across the front window of the corner shop. "Eight pounds, three ounces. Born June 21," it reads. Inside the shop everyone is smiling and the new father is handing cigars to anyone who enters as he shows Polaroid shots of a bald, patchy baby who, in his eyes, is obviously the most beautiful creature on the planet.

Birth is one of the most joyous beginnings, and one that is usually celebrated. Whenever birth occurs—an artist giving creative birth to a painting, symphony, or play, a writer giving birth to a book, a cook giving birth to a souffle, or a cat bearing a litter of tiny, mewing kittens—there is a sense of accomplishment and pride. Celebration is certainly appropriate. We experience many beginnings in our lives, some which are celebrated and honored, some which could be but are not.

There are new jobs, new homes—especially the first apartment or home of one's own—getting accepted to college, or being elected to a particular position. All are worthy of celebration; all are important transitions. We could also recognize puberty, menses, first teeth, first steps, entering adulthood, first gray hair, and the like, as beginnings of stages, as markings of time. Whether these beginnings are joyous or difficult, whether they are a cause for rejoicing or for concern, they can be given greater value with ritual.

One of the effects of ritual is to deepen our experience, to help us touch on the mythic world, and in rituals honoring beginnings we re-enact the beginning of the universe, the sowing of the seeds of existence. In comparison with this archetypal origination, getting one's first job or reaching puberty may seem inconsequential, but in our unconscious we are reliving this archetypal myth of creation with each new beginning, and this can sometimes be seen in the accompanying fear and trembling that is more appropriate to the dawn of time than to getting one's driver's license.

While the conscious experience of such changes may be limited to what we think about and sometimes feel, we live our lives on many other levels as well. We may only hear echoes of these deeper movements in our daily ploddings, or have a glance into them through a potent dream, but they are real. Ritual serves to honor not only our outward changes, but the inner, mythic motions of our souls as well.

One soul-shaking initiation we all experience is puberty. In other cultures the entry into social sexuality/adulthood has often been met with elaborate rites of passage. Puberty is an awkward and difficult time. It marks the beginning of one of the longest and rockiest transitions we may ever experience. There are approximately seven arduous years between childhood and young adulthood. These years are marked by radical and uncontrollable bodily changes, fierce, rapidly changing emotional states, an entirely new way of thinking, and an almost constant identity crisis. The teenager has one foot in the world of the child and one foot in the world of the adult, and the chasm between the worlds widens unbearably. What could possibly allay the difficulty of this excruciating roller-coaster ride? Let us not suggest that a ritual could magically solve a seven-year crisis, but let's look realistically at what is needed to make this transition easier. Often this progression is made more difficult by family members who did not receive the help they needed at this turning point in their lives, and who may be experiencing their own confusion about this changing child and the reverberating family impact.

Whenever a family member goes through a major shift, so does the family. This can raise a lot of fear. Everyone needs to recognize that the adolescent's role in the family is changing. Childhood is slowly and gradually being left behind. The teenager may at times want to fully assume the adult role with all its privileges, yet, as a child, still fear the responsibilities. It is important to support the emerging identity, however it may choose to manifest. The following is an example of a beginning ritual that could be helpful in this transition.

"Myth not only teaches and regulates, it heals and transforms. To enter into the mythical dimension is to enter into the time of primordial unity, a time when all things were and are in order. If there is a substance or aspect in man needful of redemption, healing and transformation, then contact with this other reality rejuvenates that part. The passion we refer to in talking of the need for mythical ritual arises when the two dimensions—the transpersonal and the mundane—are brought into contact with one another through the mediating act of the ritual. It is the spark which flies when two stones are struck together, the mysterium tremendum accompanying every truly religious experience, and the cure for spiritual sterility."

—Charles Ponce
Kabbalah

RITUAL ADDRESSED TO A TEENAGER

Intention: To put behind the old in a safe and gentle way, and to consider and prepare for the new.

Preparation: Perhaps you, the teenager, can arrange to spend time in your room with three large boxes, one for that which has been outgrown and is no longer needed (certain toys, games, books, or mementos), one for those things you have outgrown but with emotional value (a teddy bear or a jersey from a winning Little League game), and one for the things that are currently relevant to your life (particular records or books, jewelry, favorite art). Think about what it would mean to give away childish items to another, younger child. These would be the things for box one. Think about what it means to not want to give up certain items associated with childhood and having that be okay. These are the things to put in box two. Think about how the things for box three symbolize how you see yourself now. As you put objects in their appropriate boxes—which you may have decorated in ways that represent how you feel about yourself at these different stages of your life—you may find yourself feeling sadness, pride, anger, fear, or joy. Let these feelings happen; perhaps write about your experience in a journal. Have someone you trust with you if the feelings seem too much to handle alone. Every transition brings up emotions, often conflicting ones. Working them through is an important part of your change, of your sense of who you are, and of who you are becoming.

To help develop this sense of who you can be, plan to add items to box three that represent what might be important to how you would like to see yourself and have others see you. Ask your family members to think about something you might like and/or need to help you in your growth. It can be a tangible gift like a razor or a thesaurus, or something like guitar lessons or a certificate for a week with a half-hour extended curfew.

Manifestation: You invite your family to meet in your room at a designated time. The room should be cleaned and arranged in a way that reflects your identity. You will greet your family members and seat them around the room. Talk with them—as much as you feel comfortable with—about what is in each of the three boxes, and about your process in putting the boxes together. Particular focus should be on the third, the "present and future" box. The family should listen intently and try to discover how willing they are to support your choices. As you present the contents of the third box, each family member should be prepared to offer a gift in harmony with your needs, that may also benefit you in who you feel you are becoming as you grow toward adulthood. A gift honoring a precious part of yourself of which you may be unaware, but which others may recognize and nourish, would also be appropriate. There can then be a circle, where everyone holds hands and pledges to honor each other's struggles and growth, and offers to help make this time as easy as possible. After the circle there can be a sharing of food or drink, made more relevant if you prepared it.

Grounding: You should designate a time to give away the things in the first box to a younger child who would benefit from them. It would be useful to check the things in the second box on a monthly basis to see how much energy they still hold, and what you can pass on to someone else. It is important for the family to honor the use of the things in the third box, and for all family members to remember and honor their pledge. To help you in each of these grounding steps, you may find writing in your journal helpful, as well as speaking to your family about some of the changes you feel happening within you. Thanking them for their gifts, and letting them know how using them helps you in your transition, can keep you in touch with your process and also honor an adult mode of communication in your new life.

Like all beginning rituals, this one represents an initiation of the Self, a movement toward individuation that is yours alone, through which you must pass alone. For that reason the support of and connection with others is truly important, to help you with your solitary struggles and movements. Your efforts may remind you and those around you of the the beginning of something even larger than adolescence. You are in fact recreating in your life the labor and birthing of existence, the mythic emergence of something out of nothing, and the dawning of a new consciousness.

Mergings

Initiations, even when honored with the presence of others, are always solitary transitions. Mergings are also beginnings, but they are ones that recognize that there are some things we do not have to do alone. There are, in fact, some things we cannot do alone. When an individual has developed sufficiently to recognize distinctions between oneself and others, to realize one's own uniqueness and the uniqueness of others, then relatedness becomes possible and desirable.

In cyclical celebrations we may join with others to commemorate certain rhythms in our lives and often in the lives of all humans—the seasons, the year, and our aging, or the recognition of important turning points. These usually occur with or without our consent. In mergings, however, we make a conscious choice for the joining to happen, to benefit those involved, and possibly others.

The myth we find ourselves living in merging rituals is the union of opposites, the marriage of heaven and earth, of the sacred and the mundane. This creates something larger and of a different meaning than the expression of two entities individually. It is the establishment of relatedness where before there existed only distinction and difference and perhaps a recognition of polarity. It is a union that gives birth to a new whole that is, indeed, more than the sum of its parts.

A wedding is a striking example of this, but so is a corporate merger. In both cases two individual entities choose to unite for a certain period of time for specific purposes that will serve each party. In the case of "forced" mergings, it is still usually centered around a choice, even though it may be between the lesser of two evils. Sharing a house in order to afford a more beautiful environment when one would prefer to live alone is an illustration of such a choice.

I live in a house that has an "in-law" apartment downstairs. The house is rented to me as a whole. Therefore it is my responsibility to rent the downstairs apartment, which in some ways is a separate unit and in other ways is not. Although the apartment is sufficient unto itself, it is connected to the house by a stairway just as a basement would be. All utilities, upstairs and downstairs, are on a single meter. Parking is so limited that each household member has to check with the others if he or she is planning to have a guest drive over. And sounds—voices, music, doors closing, showers running—travel easily in a vertical as well as horizontal direction. As a result, I have had to carefully choose the downstairs tenants, as my living situation has many of the elements of communal or familial living.

When someone new moves in downstairs, no matter how I have tried to explain the situation, it generally takes time and experience for reality to sink in. We are merging two separate lifestyles, and sometimes this merging has required a series of meetings to ensure peace and harmony. Meetings and creative problem-solving can be very effective, but so too, in this situation, could a ritual.

NEW HOUSEMATES RITUAL

Intention: When two people decide to share a living space, and the emotional commitment of a couple is not part of their relationship, something is needed to provide assurance of harmony. To *prepare* to move into an apartment together, Lynn and Carol created a ritual that was very much like children playing house. In the *manifestation* of this ritual they put together a diorama of the new apartment which they named "Abode of Laughter and Beauty." They came to agreement on the purpose, use, and interior design of each room. Then they made an altar for the apartment's living room to permanently house the diorama. Every Monday evening they held house meetings before it. This served as *grounding*.

Whenever there is a merging, adjustments must be made by all individuals to achieve a healthy and balanced relationship. A romantic involvement, a partnership, or any kind of system that is formed by the ongoing interaction between different beings, is a kind of entity unto itself. A married couple, a blended family, or a team must be treated as having a reality which is part of, and yet apart from, the members that compose it.

While all rituals deal with inner or outer relationships, a merging ritual is always about specific relationships in the outer world. Accordingly, it is wise to address one of the major issues of a relationship: dependence versus independence versus interdependence. Relationships or mergings must always allow individual parties to retain their independence and distinction, even in the midst of unity. While it is valuable to be able to depend on another, it is dangerous to lose one's individual identity. That identity was struggled for and born in initiation, and if it is lost or submerged, then so too is the power of the union. In a merging ritual it is important to include a focus on separateness at the same time as celebrating coming together.

This alliance, whether based on love, common interests or goals, can be celebrated as a sharing. A ritual can offer support, affirmation of commitment, and be the model for a process to work things out.

"The function of ritual, as I understand it, is to give form to the human life, not in the way of a mere surface arrangement, but in depth."
—Joseph Campbell
Myths to Live By

Cycles

Cyclical celebrations are anniversaries. They are recurrences of notable events. Commemorating birthdays, wedding anniversaries, and holidays is almost a universal experience. Some celebrate the weekend—TGIF! Some even celebrate the end of the workday with a "happy hour." There are always dates and times that have been important to us, and when they return we may wish to honor them. A cyclical celebration can be just for the joy of having attained one more year. A ritual for a birthday or the anniversary of someone's death can be a time for us to reconnect. It is a time when we can recognize the depths of our emotional roots.

Emotions are a vital facet of being human, and they play an important part in rituals honoring cycles. The word "emotion" literally means "outward movement," which is apparent when we attend to the process of our feelings. Emotions allow us to move out of and beyond ourselves, as we experience when we fall in love. The rhythm of the seasons reminds us that we are in relationship with more than just other people. We are in moving, growing relationships with the life of the planet itself, with time, and with something more. Most religions have major holy days at seasonal turns, and cyclical rituals help us to honor and understand patterns that are larger than ourselves. They can assist us in beginning to grasp the mystery of existence, the movements and rhythms of powers beyond our control.

Power in our lives springs from becoming more conscious and increasing the relationships among the things we have learned, so that we may apply our new knowledge. At New Year's, or perhaps on birthdays, many people review the year—what they have accomplished, how they have changed—to help them set goals for the coming year. They return to the past year in a conscious way to help them in their future journeys in life. This rhythm of review, learning, and yearning moves something deeper in us that religious holidays touch upon: the myth of the eternal return. As we move through life and become more conscious of who we are, we enact this myth of returning to the beginning of time in a conscious way. Much as a child moves from undifferentiated awareness to discrimination between self and others, we as humans have moved mythically from the original One at creation to differentiating between parts of that One (into our separate selves). As each of us becomes more independent and self-aware, we gain the ability to unite with others.

In this consciously chosen reunion, we can begin to contemplate the mystery of origin and feel or recognize the presence of powers larger than ourselves. This presence may be felt in the relationship celebrated at wedding anniversaries, the vitality of nature honored at seasonal festivals, or an aspect of God that is the focus of a religious holiday. This presence is an integral part of cyclical rites, for "the World is not only re-established and regenerated, but is also sanctified by the symbolic presence of the Immortals . . . . The Immortals make it stable, healthy, rich and holy, as it was at the beginning of Time"[14]

A WINTER SOLSTICE RITUAL

Intention: Each December we hold a Yule open house, with the customary tree-trimming, gift-giving, delicious food, and warm feelings. We also include a wassail ritual. Wassail is an old Anglo-Saxon winter drink, spicy, hot, and hearty, whose name means "wholeness."

Preparation: After all the guests have arrived and socialized for a bit, four or five of us work together in the kitchen to assemble this amazing brew.

Manifestation: We carry the wassail out to the accompaniment of bells and horns and set it before the blazing fireplace. As a specially prepared log-shaped loaf of Yule bread is passed among the guests, we talk about the year, the increasing darkness from fall to winter, and the inward searching that accompanies the season. All the guests are urged to recognize an aspect of self that is no longer of use, that perhaps they have recently noticed interfering in how they would choose to live their lives. When they feel ready to release this way of being, they walk up to the hearth and throw a bit of their Yule bread into the flames, symbolically offering the outmoded part of themselves to the cleansing fire. We then toast the return of the light, and the wholeness and unity arising from the darkness and isolation of winter. We feed each other a bit of Yule bread to symbolically give, receive, and ground the gift of Spirit from the wassail, the symbol of the One.

Grounding: Discussion, singing, feasting, and merriment follow in good spirit.

Endings

In an ending, something has terminated: a relationship, a job, a project, or even a life. There may be a sense of relief or satisfaction or there may be a great sense of loss and emptiness. Suddenly being without something that was an integral part of your life can cause you to feel completely ungrounded. An ending without a sense of completion implies being unfinished rather than being settled. We have more issues to deal with when things end against our wishes than we do when we purposefully conclude something in our lives. For instance, a death, particularly of a child, leaves you to deal not only with your grief but also with the hopes and dreams you had for that person, and all the things you were never able to share with each other. The rituals of wakes and funerals are very important in helping to cope with such loss. Our culture also provides rituals such as retirement dinners or bon voyage parties for less devastating endings, but there are many other endings that could benefit from a ritual.

One such powerful situation leaving painful and possibly unresolvable issues could be returning from a business trip to find your home empty. The furniture is gone, the children are gone, your spouse is gone. Nothing remains but a few of your personal items. There is no note, and you find your spouse unavailable to you. You may not be able to ever understand what happened if you are forced to deal with this alone.

Whether the endings in our lives have unresolved elements or have intentional completion, we must still establish where we stand after the dust settles. It is important to recognize that no matter what has passed, you remain. However, who you are has changed. A large part of your experience of yourself is a composite of all your experiences, synthesized by your responses to them. If you take a moment, you may be able to recall the homes you've had over the years and what life was like at each of these places. Perhaps you can remember special moments of love given or received. Each warm memory still available to you has helped shape you, has given you strength and character, has affected your values and perceptions.

In order to recover these legacies, we need time and the ability to integrate an ending transition in a way that enriches us and honors what has ended. A ritual in the form of a memorial can support us in the important process of grieving.

Sometimes in grief, you may find an ocean of loss so deep it seems bottomless, with waves so fierce they threaten to annihilate you. When these feelings surface, your personal emotion has accessed the archetype of sorrow. You are living the myth of separation, of the loss of union with the primal, undifferentiated One: the myth of manifestation from a sacred world of relatedness into a material world of duality, the story of the Fall from Eden. This deepening of emotion is most often seen in the death of a spouse, where the original joining echoed the movement of conscious return to something larger, as discussed in the section of this chapter called Mergings. Losses of this magnitude in our lives always touch off questions about the meaning of life, and while it is difficult to explore these questions in our pain, grief does provide an opportunity to truly deepen our understanding of existence.

It is through suffering that we learn compassion, that we recognize a bond common to all people. We can experience the paradox of being united in our loss and separation, and in that experience know that we are not separate. Most religions agree that death, as the completion of life on earth, opens the possibility of a life with conscious union with the Tao, with God, with Goddess, with Spirit, that is improbable for all but a few holy persons while we are in human form. Ideally we have completed what we needed to do on earth before death ends our lives; if not, the Hindu reincarnates or the Christian spends time in purgatory before ultimate reunion with the One.

While death of a loved one brings the most full experience of this archetype, the myth is present and available to us in all losses, at all completions. Whether to deepen our experience of the archetype or to make living the myth more bearable, a ritual of completion is most valuable.

A DIVORCE RITUAL

Jenny S., during the year following her breakup with John, worked hard in therapy. With great courage she faced and coped with her loss, her rage, her guilt, her fear, her sense of powerlessness. After nine months she was feeling stronger than ever before and liking her life, her work, and her relationships. As the divorce decision approached, Jenny began feeling sad and scared. When the divorce was granted, many of her feelings from the split with John recurred or intensified. Her emotional work of the previous year made the divorce easier to deal with, but it was difficult to finalize what had happened. Together we worked out an ending ritual for her to do at home.

Preparation: Jenny took a day for herself. She cleaned the house and took a shower. She gathered the materials she had decided to use in her ritual and stated her *intention:* "Today I say good-bye to an old way of being and embrace a new life."

Manifestation: Jenny looked through pictures of their wedding and of their life together. She read over John's love letters and wept. Then she wrote a letter to the relationship they had shared giving thanks for their love and growth, and forgiveness for the hurts they had caused each other. She added this letter to those from John and tied them carefully together with a fresh ribbon. As she placed this bundle and the wedding pictures into a special box to keep the memories safe, Jenny said good-bye to their marriage and their old way of relating.

Lighting a fire in the fireplace, Jenny burned their marriage certificate. As the paper turned to fire and smoke, she set free the false beliefs and expectations she still held for the marriage and from the divorce: "I let go of the belief that I am not worthy of love. I am a loving being, deserving of love." She drank a sip of juice to help make that belief a living part of her. "I let go of expecting our relationship to make me a whole person. I am a whole person unto myself."

Grounding: When she had finished her list and her juice, she stretched and thanked God for her life, for the love she had experienced, for her strength, for the depth of her emotions and for her growth. A sadness was still present, but a fullness, and a new joy in life, was there as well.

Ending rituals can help us deal with retirement, menopause, divorce, leaving home, death, or even loss of body parts (due to an accident or to surgery such as a mastectomy). This category deals with the emotions that are most painful. The rituals must contain delicacy, patience, and compassion.

Healings

All rituals that move toward balance and increase conscious relatedness in an ethical way are healing rituals. Beginning rituals help balance the fearful transition between an old and a new way of being. Merging rituals help balance and enlarge the relationship between two separate entities. Cyclical rituals help us balance our lives by increased understanding of our relationships with time and with other larger forces. Ending rituals offer us a way to deal with the polarities of life and death; they provide us an approach to understanding questions fundamental to human nature and the nature of existence. Whenever we touch the energies that fuel and direct life, healing can happen.

When there is an imbalance in your life—a physical illness, an emotional upheaval, a way of thinking that interferes with living fully, an intensity of concern or a state of apathy that threatens your soul—ritual can help. Healing rituals offer a time for you to be fully present with the pain as well as a means to finding acceptance of it. We often spend incredible amounts of time and energy fighting what is really happening. For change to occur, we must admit what is true and accept it, even if it is unpleasant. "Health, like wholeness, is completion in individuality, and to this belongs the dark side of life as well: symptoms, suffering, tragedy, and death. *Wholeness and health therefore do not exclude these 'negative' phenomena; they are requisite for health.*"[15] When resistance to the existence of this dark side of reality is relieved, the tyranny of pain diminishes, and change can occur. Balance can then be restored.

A RITUAL FOR PLANETARY HEALING

Preparation: A few of us gather weekly at noon, the time of the most light. We sit quietly in a circle, focusing on our breath, allowing distractions to be released while exhaling and strength and centeredness to enter when inhaling.

Manifestation: The leader for the week lights a white candle in the center of our circle and states our *intention:* that we are gathered here to promote healing on and of our planet earth, for the good of all. We stand and join hands, and the leader guides us through a meditation in which we each become filled with light, acknowledging our individual wounds and imbalances, then imagining ourselves well and whole. We let the light expand from us and fill and embrace our circle, and we speak the names of those people we know are in need of healing, imagining them in the center of the light circle, seeing them move toward balance. We pray in this way for world leaders, global areas of strife or injustice, pollution—each time imagining the way things are now, and then the way they can be. After this, we lift up our arms and send this globe of healing energy out into the universe, asking that it be used where it might best be of service. We close by giving thanks to Spirit and hugs to each other.

Grounding: The sense of peace and healing from the ritual is carried home with each of the participants; we can call on it throughout the week to help those qualities become part of our daily activities.

This ritual often leaves us feeling in love with the world, and there are definite similarities between healing and love. They are not things we can create, but things that happen to us and through us, states that we are blessed to experience. Love and healing are energies that exist, awaiting access, and when the proper avenues are created for them, these energies pour through and grace us with their expression. Ritual can be such an avenue.

---

14. Mircea Eliade, op. cit., p. 208.

15. James Hillman, *Suicide and the Soul* (Dallas, TX: Spring Publications, Inc., 1964), p. 125.

Chapter 5

The Process of Ritual

The process of ritual follows the same basic stages we experience in life. These stages of unfolding are paralleled by the seasons and their changes. In spring, the increased warmth of the earth awakens seeds to life, and the sprouts struggle upward. During summer the nourishment of the sun, water, and earth help the seedlings find a more mature form, and the plants may produce exquisite flowers. After pollination, in the fall, fruit drops to the ground or is harvested. In winter we eat the fruits and save the seeds, or the fallen seeds find their way into the earth to await the recurrence of spring.

Each of the seasons and each age of a plant—seedling, sapling, flower, and fruit—is unique. But when we look at the whole cycle of the year or of a plant's growth, we see the larger beauty of balance and rhythm inherent in creation and in life.

When we create something—a dinner, a painting, a ritual—we go through the same process. We are inspired, and we bring that inspiration into creation by thinking and planning. As we work with our ideas and the feelings they evoke, the inspiration finds a skeletal form. That form provides a framework to be fleshed out. This is all part of the preparation process, and the manifestation process echoes the same stages. Let's look at how this process might be expressed in the example of preparing a dinner for some friends.

Preparation: An old friend is in town with his new girlfriend. You want to cook dinner for them as a way to honor your friend and welcome his partner. This is the inspiration for the dinner. You think about the kinds of food he likes, rummage through cook-books for recipes, and toy with ideas for table settings. You decide that while you'd like to serve filet mignon, your budget is better suited to beef stroganoff. It might be nice to create more of an inviting atmosphere with music and flowers, and you consider the mood that would be most appropriate.

As you play with these ideas, different feelings begin to emerge. Perhaps you're nervous about what kind of impression you'll make on his new love. What if you don't like her? Are you jealous? Will your friends think you don't value them enough to take them out to dinner? You worry a little, then decide to put candles on the dinner table for elegance and warmth. You work through each of your doubts and fears until you are back to your original intention of welcoming these people into your home and into your heart. Finally you begin to feel more relaxed about creating a successful evening, then—Oh no! You remember the girl-friend is a committed vegetarian. This requires more research to decide on a suitable entree. It's clear now that the plans you made in the creative stage are taking form.

Manifestation: Your next step is to bring these forms into mani-festation. You make a grocery list, make special stops at the bak-ery and flower stand after the market, and return home to prepare. The afternoon is spent cleaning, polishing, arranging the table, and cooking. When things are almost complete, you take some time to shower and dress. When your guests arrive, you greet them genially and escort them into the living room for hors d'oeuvres. This is the physical beginning of your dinner. As you move into the dining room for the meal, you further the intention and mood of the evening by lighting the candles and making a toast to friendships old and new. During the dinner your rapport increases with the sharing of good food, a bottle of wine, and warm conversation. After the meal is over, everyone lingers over coffee, listening to music and talking. Eventually the evening draws to a close.

Grounding: As you say good-bye, you all promise to keep in touch. The dinner has been successful, and you feel good as you clean up. The next day you talk with your friend about the eve-ning, and make plans for the three of you to get together again.

PREPARATION

Preparing a ritual involves four stages: clarifying the intention; planning; emotional process; and physical preparation. The steps of each stage are described here, and outlined in the Ritual Worksheet in Chapter 9.

Clarifying the Intention

The primary difference between the dinner described above and a ritual dinner is the conscious carrying and implementation of the intention through each stage of the process. Identifying, clarifying, and developing the intention is the first stage of preparation. These are some questions to be considered:

Why are you thinking about doing a ritual? What has happened, is happening, or is about to happen that inspires you?

What is the purpose of this ritual? What do you want it to accomplish? What kind of mood do you want created? Whom will this ritual affect? How will this ritual benefit the participants?

What myth or archetypal journey might be similar to the inspiration for your ritual?

Is the aim of this ritual realistic? If you find you have a lot of different goals, you may need to do several different rituals.

Of the five ritual categories, beginnings, mergings, cycles, endings, or healings, which seems most appropriate? How?

Go to Chapter 4 and reread the section on the category you have chosen.

Make sure you can clearly state your intention.

Planning

Having clarified your intention, you now progress to the planning stage. This stage encompasses choosing different symbols and actions for each Element of ritual (Earth, Air, Fire, Water, and Essence; see Chapter 6), creative design, and logistics.

Now that you have determined what kind of ritual you wish to create, you need to decide on the following:

Who should participate in this ritual, and why? Do the people who will be involved in the ritual have the same aim? What purpose do they have in common? If you do this ritual alone, are you ambivalent about achieving your goal? If so, what belief or idea do you need to let go of or work through? Is there anyone who might be touched by but would not benefit from the performance of this ritual? If so, how can you shift the intention so that your aim is clear and no one could be hurt?

What specifically do you want to recognize, honor, support, or heal?

When would be most appropriate to enact this ritual?

Where would be the most fitting setting for the ritual to take place?

How will this ritual benefit and affect the participants?

How much or how little needs to be done?

CHOOSING SYMBOLS

Chapter 6, The Elements of Ritual, will give you a thorough understanding of the four Elements—Earth, Air, Fire, and Water—and of the unifying principle of Essence. By combining this information with what you learned about symbols from Chapter 3, Myth, History, and Symbols, you should be able to choose symbols that are meaningful, powerful, relevant, and that bring a sense of balance and wholeness to your ritual. For now, just be aware that Earth is generally associated with the body, the direction of north, the Jungian function of sensation, and in the Tarot, with the Princesses. The grounding stage of a ritual, and ending rituals, fall within the realms of Earth.

The Element of Air corresponds to the mind, the direction of east, the function of thinking, and the Princes in the Tarot. Rituals of merging, and the planning stage of a ritual, relate to Air.

Fire generally relates to what is called spirit or inspiration, which we are going to call energy. Fire also corresponds to the direction of south, the function of intuition, and the Kings. Rituals which honor beginnings, and the ritual stage of inspiration, fit into this category.

Water's relationships are emotions, the west, feelings, and the Queens. The stages of emotional process and blessings belong with Water, as do cyclical types of rituals.

The fifth Element of Spirit—here called Essence—is not included in all systems. We suggest this Element be understood as that which is the foundation for and yet transcends all the other Elements. Essence is present in the ritual as a whole and in the larger energies that enter the ceremony. Healing rituals correspond to the Element of Essence.

When you have a sense of what symbols you would like to incorporate into your ritual, you can focus more on the creative design.

CREATIVE DESIGN

Ritual is a performance art. Allowing yourself to have artistic license, to let ideas flow no matter how extravagant or odd they may seem, will put you in the most creative space. You may need to start by recalling what a traditional ceremony for this occasion includes (if there is one), and spin off from there. For example a birthday party celebrates the anniversary of the day someone is born. People are invited who are glad to know that this person has made it successfully through another year. There is generally a cake with a candle to mark each year that has passed and one extra to grow on. Blowing out the candles and making a wish for the coming year is related to taking the strength and wisdom acquired over the past years and creating a positive intention with it that will be used inwardly as a guiding light. At children's parties, along with the birthday song may come birthday spankings—one for each year—related to the pain of growing. Lastly, there are gifts which are an expression of love from each of the guests.

An example of a birthday ritual follows:

Preparation: For my fortieth birthday, I decided to do a ritual that would include some of the standard symbols, but with the *intention* of expressing what being forty meant to me. I decided to rent a space that was large enough to accommodate all of my friends and my family—everyone who had supported me through the years and was still in my life. Each person was asked to bring, as a "giveaway," an item that represented their personal gift to the world or something they liked about themselves.

Manifestation: During the ritual, everyone stood encircling a round loaf of bread, which held a single candle to represent unity. I expressed my feelings about my belief that the first half of life involves discovering something about who you are and what your gifts are, and the second half has more of an outward focus, sharing your gifts to make a better world. I described what I felt my gift was and explained the symbolic object I'd brought to represent it. I then passed my gift to the person to my left, who did the same with their gift, and so on around the circle until all gifts were shared. We then did a short meditation, holding hands, focusing on how, by being who we are and sharing it with those around us, we create something that continues to grow and spread. We mentally released any limitations that might keep us from sharing our personal gifts or resources. Finally we all stepped forward to take and eat a piece of the bread, which symbolized the grounding and nurturing of what had been shared.

Grounding: The rest of the ritual included many of the traditional elements of a birthday celebration, but the way it had been personalized gave it a meaning that has stayed with me to this day. When the ritual you want to perform has no model that already exists, you may still find similar elements in other ceremonies that might give you ideas. Basically you need to consider:

How will you start?

Will there be music, poetry, chants, readings, speeches, or meditations?

Will there be a cleansing of the people or of the space?

Are you including the use of food or wine, for feasting or offerings?

How will all the symbols best be included?

Will there be any particular artistic event, such as body-painting, mask-making, incense-crafting, the making of a ritual object, or something along those lines?

How will the pace be sustained?

What kind of ending would be fitting?

These kinds of questions need to be considered, keeping in mind the intention and the symbols you have chosen. As you sketch out your ideas, you'll find that the next section enters the picture.

LOGISTICS

Here you want to consider each person's role and responsibilities in the ritual, plan the gathering and organizing of materials, and work out the timing. You may want to have a planning meeting with the participants if each is to have a very active role. If you are going to be doing most of the leading, it may only be necessary to contact the guests, discuss what they need to bring, get an idea of how they will participate, and then coordinate everything. If others are to be a part of the ritual, getting feedback from them will give you valuable information about what to add or delete.

If you are performing this ritual alone, you still need to spend some time with this stage, as the preparation stages all enhance the power of the ritual itself.

Emotional Process

The limitations you dealt with in your planning stage may have raised some emotions, such as anger, frustration, excitement, or doubt. In every creative process you run into blocks, and creating a ritual is no exception. This is an excellent opportunity to take stock of yourself, to see if your original goals remain the same, and to explore any doubts or fears that may have come forth. If the ritual you are planning is a celebration, you may find yourself tapping into a lot of feelings that are positive and warm. Should the celebration be for yourself, however, beware of the old "Do I really deserve this?" plague.

When the ritual is to help deal with illness, death, or some painful ending, it is more likely that some difficult feelings will emerge. Dealing with these feelings is a cleansing and part of the healing process of ritual. It is important to acknowledge and honor whatever emotions arise. You can include symbolic events in the ritual that will assist you in releasing some of the more difficult feelings. This can be done by safely burning or burying paper that names certain things or feelings, or even by burning or burying certain objects or photographs from which you wish to be freed. Remember, each of the Elements offers symbolic ways to find release.

Physical Preparation

This is the time to actually gather the necessary materials, set up, and make sure all the details worked out in the planning stage are coming together. You may want a checklist to ensure that each of the necessary items is covered. This stage feels a lot like packing for a vacation, and in a sense it is quite similar. You are taking all the essential things to go away to another time and place where your ordinary reality is temporarily set aside, and everything is designed to offer healing or renewal.

MANIFESTATION

The manifestation stage is the performance of the ritual. There are four parts to this: creating a sacred space; declaration and enactment of the intention; invocation of larger energies; and blessing and closure.

Creating a Sacred Space

After all the materials have been gathered and prepared as needed, the space in which the ritual will be performed must be defined and consecrated. If the space is indoors, you might want to clear away some of the things that ordinarily identify its use. You can clean or straighten up, and then decorate the space or set up the things you plan to use during the ritual. A typical cleansing involves burning incense, or some dried herbs like sage or sweetgrass, and letting the smoke fill the room, changing the energy with its pungence. If you are performing your ritual outdoors, you may need to delineate the area to contain the ritual with rocks, chairs, or something that helps you feel a sense of enclosure. Describing the sacred space within the shape of a circle helps induce a sense of wholeness and unity. Whether the ritual is to be indoors or outdoors, there should be some indication that when one enters the ritual space things are different and special in comparison to the surrounding area. This can be partially accomplished with some form of ceremonial entry.

Declaration and Enactment of Intention

Once the ritual space is formally entered and places are taken, the mood of the ritual is formed, and the intention is declared. Many formal events begin with a greeting or welcome, followed by some form of introduction that includes the purpose or intention. In a wedding, for example, the officiant often states, "Dearly beloved, we are gathered here today to witness and celebrate the joining in marriage of these two people." One of the most common places we see this structure is on television. The function of the host or emcee of a TV show greets and welcomes the viewers, audience, and possibly the guests, and then proceeds to describe the events that are to follow. The show is then presented according to the stated outline.

And so it is with a ritual. You have already determined what you want your ritual to include, and have developed a plan and some form of agenda. This is where all of these things are carried out.

Invocation and Direction of Larger Energies

One of the things that makes a ritual different from a TV show is that the mistress or master of ceremonies is conducting a sacred ceremony.

To assist in the process of shifting from the secular to the sacred, we invoke energies that are greater than ourselves to be with us during the rite. Even though these energies may be called from within, as when connecting with the God of your heart, or your sense of your spirit, they are transpersonal rather than personal. You can also call for the expression of an archetype, such as Venus, the goddess of love, to support an anniversary, or an ancestor or historical figure to bring, say, the energy of the wise elder. An Element, quality, or direction can be called upon with a formal greeting and beckoning: "Hail, O East, direction of sunrise, new light, and beginnings. . ." or, "Mother Earth, lend us your strength, support, and nurturing as we. . ." In a traditional religious ceremony we call upon God, Allah, the Creator of the universe, or whatever/whomever is believed in, to bless and guide us in the ritual.

Energies can be invoked with words, or with actions. The

"The idea of a receptacle is an archetypal idea ... It is the idea of the magic circle which is drawn round something that has to be prevented from escaping or protected against hostile influences ... When the ground-plan for a city was set out, there used to be a ritual walk or ride round the circumference in order to protect the place within ... This structure of a circle within a square is called in Sanskrit a Mandala ... The symbol of the Mandala has exactly this meaning of a holy place, a 'temenos' to protect the centre ..."

—C. G. Jung
Analytical Psychology, Its Theory and Practice

simple act of lighting a candle can represent bringing in Spirit, or light, as a conscious force. Whatever you decide to do, it is important to hold the intention of what you wish to accomplish as you take this step. It is also important to remember that calling in larger energies can be intimidating for some people. After all, you are calling on a force that in some way has a greater, or at least a different kind of, power from the one you are generally aware of having yourself. Do this with honor and respect, and do not attempt to call forth anything that might be associated with anger, fear, or danger. It is unlikely that you will confront danger if you do not provoke it.

Blessing and Closure

The final stages of the ritual confirm and summarize as well as complete what has been done. A semi-traditional wedding ceremony exemplifies this:

> May these two find in each other the love for which all seek. May they grow in understanding and compassion. May the home they establish together be such a place of love that many will find there a neighbor and a friend . . . . Inasmuch as _____ and _____ have consented together in marriage and have witnessed the same before this company, and thereto have pledged their faith to the other, and have declared the same by joining hands, and by giving and receiving a ring, they are husband and wife together. Those whom love hath joined together, let none put asunder.

Certainly all endings need not be as formal. In fact, in a ritual that is totally personal, with no one else in attendance, you may choose not to speak out loud at all. Many rituals are completed with only symbolic actions, such as leaving food as an offering, extinguishing candles, burning a photograph, ending a musical piece, or getting a hug from everyone in attendance.

Another consideration at this stage is: What do you do with the energies you have invoked? This is an appropriate occasion to thank the forces that be for attending, guarding, or assisting, and then release them to return to their own realm. You might also ask that the love and good feelings shared by those present be carried out to touch the hearts of others in their lives.

A simple rule for this part of the process might be: Whatever is opened must be closed; whatever is called in must be released; whatever is started must be brought full circle to completion.

GROUNDING

Breakdown and Evaluation

The last stage of the ritual is carried over into the beginning stages of completion. The physical area must be seen to, the sacred space returned to normal, and the ritual tools put away. As you attend to the physical acts of completion, you may notice that a somewhat different *you* is acting. The shifts that have occurred in you or in the other participants should be evaluated. You can assess the changes that have taken place by considering questions such as:

What was especially moving, exciting, frightening, healing, affirming, or provocative?

Have any of the relationships shifted, such as: with those present, an individual with their inner self, or an individual with someone not present?

How, specifically, do you feel?

What, if anything, was learned?

Sometimes it is difficult to articulate the changes until some time has passed. Keep monitoring yourself over the next days and weeks to note anything that feels related to your ritual work. Journal entries can be especially useful for this aspect.

You can also benefit from evaluating the ritual itself. Consider the objects used as symbols, the performance, and the design to determine what worked well and what could be improved or discarded. Each ritual will help you to be better prepared for the next.

Integration and Actualization

The last stage of completion is to follow through with any inspiration you may have received from the ritual. You may have discovered something in the course of the ritual that can be carried over into your daily life. When you are caught up in the energy and magic of a ceremony, profound feelings or insights may arise. The ritual may even have afforded you the opportunity to experience some new and welcomed behaviors. Although the sacred quality of the ritual may lead you to believe that what has occurred in that time belongs only to that time, the truth is that the rareness of the occasion may have left you with special and valuable gifts.

A healing ritual might teach you that you need some time for meditation, or to be listened to. A ritual for beginnings may have taught you new ways to deal with fear. Being the leader of a ritual may have taught you to recognize your power from the ability to empower others. Whatever you learned, the value increases as you find ways to incorporate these gifts into your life.

Chapter 6

The Elements of Ritual

We have spoken repeatedly about the importance of balance. The purpose of ritual is to increase balance and connection within ourselves, with each other, with the world, and with the subtle but powerful rhythms and energies of the cosmos and the spiritual realm. To achieve balance in a complex whole, it is necessary to be familiar with the component parts, to recognize the way each is or can be expressed, and to know when one Element or another is preventing equilibrium.

We are all physical, feeling, thinking, inspired human beings. Each of us tends to be more at ease with the qualities of some of these aspects than others. When we meet people who are working to develop those areas of themselves with which they are less facile and have achieved a fair balance, we say they are "well rounded" or "well adjusted" or that they have "gotten themselves together."

An imbalanced individual would be a "Mr. Spock" type—someone with extraordinary analytical ability, incredibly brilliant, yet with an apparent lack of feeling that makes him seem not quite human. You may know someone who can express amazing depth of feeling through music or painting, but trips over her tongue when trying to converse. How about a person so involved in the dreams of what might be or of what could happen that they are boggled by the practical world and the minutiae of daily living?

An individual who is as imbalanced as those in the exaggerated examples above is like a table with one short leg. In a healing ritual, helping one be more aware of their essential imbalances may be the first step toward wholeness.

During times of transition, we may find ourselves out of balance in other ways. A difficult passage may catapult us into an

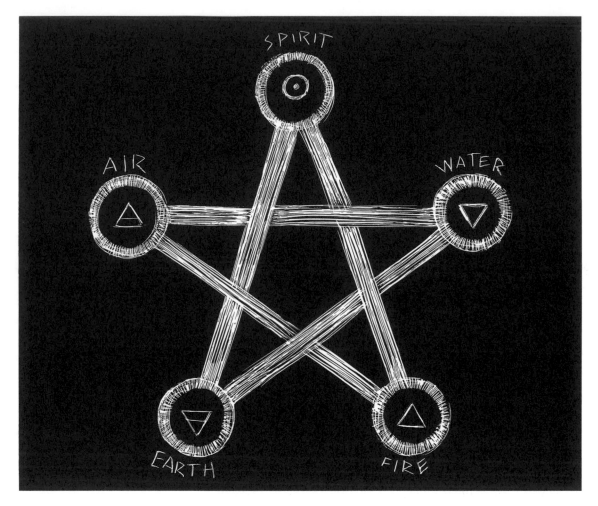

overwhelming emotional state, or it may have the opposite effect.
Some people are so afraid of their feelings that after a crisis,
which may cause them to shut down and become very rational
and contained, as we all have a tendency to do, they hide within
that protected condition. The different inner states have correspondences in Elements, seasons, directions, symbols, colors, and
more. A ritual provides an allegorical mirror in which the balance
created in the ceremony can reflect on our inner state.

These are some of the correspondences that can be symbolically used to help create balance:

East	South	West	North
spring	summer	autumn	winter
Air	Fire	Water	Earth
infancy	youth	middle age	old age
dawn	midday	evening	night
crescent moon	full moon	waning moon	new moon
thinking	intuition	feeling	sensation

You will notice that there are only four Elements represented in this chart. The fifth Element, Essence, is the energy that permeates all nature and represents the wholeness or unity itself.

We experience the Elements daily in our lives. The sun (Fire) and the stars at night radiate their light and heat, which travel through our atmosphere (Air) and the oceans (Water), which cover a large portion of the solid world (Earth).

The relationship among these four Elements is Essence, which we perceive in the interactions and movements arising from Elemental relationships. A sunset, for example, is the relationship of light from the sun (Fire) moving through the atmosphere (Air) and clouds (Water) and registering on the retinas of our eyes (Earth). This physical sensation (Earth) evokes feelings (Water)—"Wow!"—and thoughts (Air)—"How beautiful!"—in us. We may also be inspired (Fire) by the sight to say a prayer of thanks, to try and capture the image on canvas, or to just carry the energy of the event with us through the rest of the evening.

The Elements are ever present in our lives. Increasing our awareness of them allows us to more fully experience a sense of sacredness, which is vital to ritual. Let's explore each Element in greater detail.

"The pentacle is the four elements plus the fifth—essence. And it is the five stages of life, each an aspect of the Goddess: 1. Birth ... (beginning), 2. Initiation ... (individuation), 3. Love ... (union), 4. Repose ... (integration), and 5. Death ... (letting go)."

Starhawk
The Spiral Dance

Fire (Intuition) △

The Element of Fire in the Jungian typology is associated with intuition. Through this function we experience visions or new possibilities. The tendency of intuition is to allow us "to gain a total impression of a situation and also a sense for where it is leading, that is, for what may become of it."[16] Intuition leads us to the quest. "Because he [the intuitive or fiery type] is always seeking out new possibilities, stable conditions suffocate him. He seizes new objects or situations with great intensity, sometimes with extraordinary enthusiasm . . . . "[17] You might say that each new situation is an initiation into another level of growth.

This kind of fiery inspiration is also related to spirit. The fifth Element, Essence, may be seen as Spirit too, but with a capital S. Fire may be understood as the first emanation from the ineffable essence of Spirit. It is trans-temporal. The spirit of Fire can be expressed simply as warmth, or more dramatically as passion. Fire also symbolizes faith, will, force, and courage. In a ritual this might be expressed with a cone of power, where the energy is increasingly raised within the circle until the force is so great that there is a climactic release and subsequent cleansing.

"Getting the Holy Spirit" is a way Fire is embodied in the religious rituals used by some churches, such as the Pentecostal. Raising the kundalini is another way of incorporating the fiery energy of spirit.

To symbolize this energy in a ritual, a wand may be used, or candles, or a fire used for cleansing or burning away things that must be released. Actions may include anything that inflames or inspires. In a ritual that represents beginnings, Fire might symbolize leadership, inspiration, or the quest. The qualities of passion or enthusiasm might be the focus in a merging ritual. A cyclical celebration might honor aspiration or the challenge of another turn of time's wheel. Will or strength may be evoked to help with an ending. Healing rituals might benefit from Fire being expressed as optimism or purification.

Air (Mind) △

Our minds provide us with the experience of objectivity and discrimination. Through the mind we are able to notice differences, to make comparisons, to categorize, and to name things. You might say we look at the relationships among things. We can gain information, understanding, and clarity using our mind or our intellect. This process of thought is associated with Air. Perhaps this is because our thoughts are so much like the sky—either clear and open; clear with small, white clouds streaking across or drifting casually by; or dark and heavy, tormented by threatening gray-black thunderclouds. Our thoughts may be like the rushing winds of a tornado, expressing our rage, or blinding us with our confusion. The Air is also a medium which carries the expressions of thought as the waves of sound or as the signals from radio or television.

In a ritual, the Element of Air is expressed in communication, ideas, meditations, and possibilities. In time, Air is associated with the future. Methods of expression can be speech, song, story-telling, poetry, chanting, and drumming. Air can be symbolized by things representative of thought, such as books, or by objects that find the air as home: incense, feathers, or petals, which in a ritual can be tossed to the wind. Swords or knives cut through or discriminate, and so also betoken Air. The drums that produce the powerful rhythmic sound waves that provide the vehicle for journeying can also symbolize Air.

When we symbolically denote Air in a ritual, we do so for a number of reasons. In honoring or invoking Air, we are asking the qualities represented by it to be available to us. In a ritual that falls into the category of beginnings, Air may be used to represent original thinking and help tap into new ideas. In a merging ritual, Air may be used to let us recognize the differences between the individuals and create ways to understand and communicate that will allow the distinctions to remain. Air can help us to see the gestalt, or larger picture, in which all parts have a place. Using the Element of Air in a cyclical celebration can help us reflect on the past and understand patterns that occur. In an ending ritual, Air can be used symbolically for release when it is necessary, or to help remember, when retaining a part of what has been lost is what is needed. Bringing Air into a healing may mean undoing the negative mental processes that created defeat, futility, indecisiveness, overanalysis, or self-criticism.

Water (Feelings) ▽

Our feelings afford us a sense of rhythm and relatedness. Sometimes, looking at a sleeping child, or seeing a sky streaked with the reds and oranges of a setting sun, you can be touched as if you've been blessed by some unseen force. That feeling can move you out of a sense of isolation into one of connection with other people or with nature. When you have that recognition of sentience with another, you may experience joy and love; when you feel distant or separated from a person you love, you may become hurt or angry. Even anger is in relation to someone or something, and it usually comes when the known rhythm of that relationship has been upset.

Feelings, like Water, can have many forms. Some are held obscure and protected in hidden parts of our psyches, like water that has seeped down to the deepest level and formed a dark pool. Cold, contained feelings can give the effect of ice; slow anger may seem like steam; overwhelming grief, sadness, or helplessness can whip you about like a violent hurricane; and the feelings of contentment that come from being well loved may remind you of the clear, sparkling, reflective qualities of a pristine lake. And just as you can look into the smooth surface of a body of water and see the likeness of an image, so Water symbolizes illusion. It connects us with the past.

In rituals we use water and other liquids to indicate feelings. We also find feeling present in the movements and emotions of the participants and in the cadence and rhythm of the process of the ritual itself. Chalices are often used as a symbol for Water. Washing or sprinkling water for cleansing is a common ritual expression. Water is the receptive Element, and may be used in beginning rituals to express openness to something new. In a merging ritual, Water may be used as a symbol of harmony, or empathy. A cyclical celebration can employ the Element of Water to convey the sense of flow that occurs as we pass through time. When honoring an ending, the Element of Water might signify assimilation, sentiment, or sensitivity. The qualities of compassion and nurturing can be brought into a healing ritual through the Element of Water.

Earth (Body) ▽

We are earthbound because of our bodies. Of the Elemental expressions, Earth is the least able to move freely. It must be treated with honor and patience. There is no doubt that our thoughts, feelings, and intuitions are commonly held in check by the physical process that contains them. Our bodies are vehicles of experience. They provide a way for us to express ourselves and to ground or manifest our energies, in addition to allowing access to the experience of sensation. Our involvement with Earth gives us a sense of the present.

The earth itself is recognized as a great body of land, or as the fruitful Mother Earth. This was exemplified by the Romans who engraved their tombstones with the phrase *Mater genuit, Mater recepit,* which translates as "the Mother bore me, the Mother took me back."

The information we have of ancient peoples and their ways from monuments cleft on the earth, cut into the earth, or sealed within the heart of it, illustrates one of the reasons that the Element of Earth is associated with heritage, history, and the legacies of our ancestors. Even our physical bodies give indication of our ancestry through genetic traits.

The information we have from the past guides us in building the present and the future. Building is associated with the Earth, as are the qualities associated with creation and construction. So patience, endurance, determination, and practicality are all Earthy considerations.

When we wish to represent the Element of Earth in a ritual, the concepts of grounding, stability, solidity, and security can be accented. You might choose symbolic objects like stones, metals, crystals, or food. A ritual to honor beginnings may want to emphasize determination or work on grounding the emerging energies. In a cyclical celebration, you may want to explore the idea of what has been gained over time. You may wish to highlight patience in a merging ceremony. The Element of Earth can target heritage or legacy in rituals for endings. For healing, stability can be addressed through Earth. Earth can be symbolically represented in many ways—through the making of fetishes or talismans, with masks, feasting, planting, harvesting, or sculpting.

Essence (Life Force Energy) ☉

The function of Essence in a ritual is to create balance and unity. Since this is also the function of ritual, Essence is present in the ritual itself. Consciously blending the four Elements of a ritual in a balanced way also gives rise to Essence—the whole that is more than the sum of its parts.

Even though Essence is present in the ritual itself, it is useful—we think vital—to include a symbolic expression of this life force energy. As it is made sensible, the reality of a presence otherwise easily disregarded can have profound impact. Recognizing Essence is the vehicle toward transcendence. Although there may be many names for this quintessential energy—prana, chi, ether, Akasha, Spirit, God, the Tao, to name some—this force, so fundamental, is still just an abstract principle to most.

Therefore we symbolically realize the energy with a cauldron, in which all the other Elements are mixed and transformed, by the color black of the undifferentiated void, or the whiteness of the colors all returned and blended. Light is the archetypal symbol for Essence because it allows us to see (to become conscious) and because it radiates equally in all directions (unites all it touches). When people have spiritual experiences, they are often said to have become "enlightened." Among many cultures the symbol for Essence and the symbol for the sun is the same: a circle with a dot in the center. Sometimes Essence is represented solely by the dot, the *bindu,* which is the point of origin and return. Alternatively, Essence may be depicted by the circle, the perfect symbol for wholeness and unity.

Finding a way to symbolize the Elements in a ritual is important. We have given you some general and universal correspondences for them. You will want to express other things in symbolic

"God is an intelligible sphere—a sphere known to the mind, not to the senses—whose center is everywhere and whose circumference is nowhere."

—Joseph Campbell
The Power of Myth

form in your rituals as well. Cirlot's *A Dictionary of Symbols* is a good place to look for ideas. You will also benefit by knowing how to recognize or create symbols that have particular meaning for you.

PERSONALIZING SYMBOLS

You and your life and your needs are unique. At the same time that you are different and distinctive, due largely to the total of your experiences and how they affected you, those very experiences may in many ways be common to others. Think of your family of origin—over the years you have found certain similarities with them, and certain important differences.

You may have retained the values and meanings of some of your family's symbols, but you may have found things that have particular significance for you—a genre of music, a style of dress, the writing of a certain author, something you like to collect, being around water. Things that have special meaning for you become part of your personal symbology.

We knew a woman who was very involved with her home. To her, home was a sanctuary. She felt that her dwelling and her innermost self were reflections of each other that had reciprocal influence. When she felt confusion in her life, she would put her home in order. Fortunately, she lived in a studio apartment, as she would systematically clean and straighten everything around, from cupboard to closet. Upon completion of her ritual task, she would sit back and bask in the beauty and order of it all, and feel that she had regained a sense of balance. She used her personal symbology and also archetypal symbology, for the home is usually considered a representation of the Self. The cleaning and straightening was a cleansing on a symbolic level. The intensity of her involvement brought a sense of inspiration, and relaxing in the center of her ordered space allowed integration, equilibrium and harmony.

With practice you can learn to recognize the things in your life that impact you most, that you use symbolically, or with which you identify. And these can be translated into your ritual signature.

ELEMENT SELECTION GUIDE

To assist you in choosing appropriate Elemental symbols for your rituals, you can use the following tables, which contain possible actions, objects, colors, and sounds for each of the Elements. You will undoubtedly find more symbols to add to these lists. Let these tables be a starting point for your exploration into how the Elements take part in your life.

EARTH ▽

Objects

- solid, sturdy objects or shapes, such as cubes, globes, or squares
- stones, metals, crystals, wood
- foods: breads, grains, meat, fruits, mushrooms, other hearty foods
- clothing: coats, capes, other warm heavy clothes; rough, mottled textures, such as wool
- scents: heavy, musky odors; the smell of earth, a forest floor, or baking bread

Actions

- stillness, or slow, steady, deliberate motions
- lying, sitting, or squatting
- the motions of digging, planting, and harvesting
- eating—ingestion and digestion
- moving to each of the four quadrants in your ritual circle

Colors

- earth tones: browns, blacks, russets, olive greens, and yellows
- darkness, or a dim, steady light
- nighttime

Sounds

- silence, or the pauses between sounds
- low, deep tones; slow, steady rhythms
- bass instruments, such as drum, fiddle, oboe, tuba
- speech that refers to the body, the world, or actions

WATER ▽

Objects

- water itself, other liquids
- cups and other liquid containers, crescent shapes
- sea shells, starfish, images of fish, dolphins, and other water inhabitants
- foods: libations, clear broths
- clothing: smooth, flowing textures or materials such as silk
- scents: rain, sea air, water lilies

Actions

- fluid, graceful, rhythmic motions
- actions that denote the giving and receiving aspects of water: pouring, drinking, washing
- dancing, swaying

Colors

- blues, blue-greens, silvers
- filtered or indirect light, gently changing
- twilight

Sounds

- melodious, flowing sounds
- rhythmic chanting, rushing water, waves, rain
- vibraphone, harp, rhythm section, alto pitch
- poetry or singing, speech that appeals to the emotions

AIR △

Objects

- air and wind, round shapes
- feathers, fans, incense, pinwheels, books, and pens
- foods: light desserts such as puff pastry; champagne and other sparkling drinks
- clothing: light and free-fitting
- clear and delicate scents

Actions

- quick, light motions
- lifting up or offering up
- speaking or reading

Colors

- sky blue, blues, and whites
- bright but indirect light, increasing in intensity; electric lighting
- the morning sun

Sounds

- sound itself
- clear, high-pitched tones; rapid, precise, light rhythms
- the rushing wind, rustling sounds
- wind chimes, flutes and woodwinds, rattles, bells, or drums
- speech and laughter; words that direct the thoughts; appeals to reason and logic

FIRE △

Objects

- fire, flame, candles, lamps and fireplaces, torches, matches, sparklers and fireworks; triangular shapes
- foods seasoned with hot spices such as cayenne, salsa, tobasco or curry; hot foods and drinks
- clothing: light and warm
- scents: sharp, tangy smells like cinnamon; odors from a fire

Actions

- darting, rapid movements
- lighting a fire or a candle; burning or sacrificing something

Colors

- reds, oranges and yellows
- bright, direct light, steady like the noon-time sun, or a flickering fire, or candle-light

Sounds

- arpeggios, and staccato rhythms
- the crackling of a fire, violins and other high-pitched strings, soprano instruments
- enflaming speeches, stating the intention, invocations and appeals to Spirit

ESSENCE ☉

Objects

- central altar, candle, lantern or lamp
- the ritual circle

Actions

- standing in the center of the circle
- holding hands in a circle

Colors

- brightness; light itself

Sounds

- sounds of pitch higher than human hearing
- a solitary clear soprano note, a choir's single voice
- instruments with a lingering echo, such as Tibetan bells produce
- in speech, giving thanks for what has been received from Spirit during the invocation

---

16. June Singer, *Boundaries of the Soul* (New York: Anchor Press, 1973), p. 191.
17. Joseph Campbell, editor, *The Portable Jung* (New York, Viking Press, 1971), p. 223.

Chapter 7

Crafting and Consecrating Tools

While you are considering how you wish to bring each of the Elements into your ritual and what symbols represent you, your needs, and your goals, it is important to recall one of the keys to achieving power through ritual expression: The ordinary is replaced by the extraordinary. Let's compare the creation of the extraordinary in a ritual with the transformation of the common to the magical in a theatrical production.

For the first script reading, the actors and actresses sit in chairs and recite their lines. A set designer creates a ground plan for the staging, and in the subsequent script-readings the blocking is done. This is where places are literally blocked out. Props are gradually added and the set is progressively built. At each of these stages the magic of creativity can be found, but the transformation to another reality is yet to come. What we are looking for may be experienced during the dress rehearsal, but it is not until the night of the first performance, the night everyone has been working toward, with costumes and makeup on, with the set, music, and lighting flawless, and with the audience waiting in anticipation on the other side of the curtain, that the shift occurs. The curtain rises and everyone succumbs to the spell and enters another world.

For the theater company, each step is more evocative. An actor becomes involved with a role not only through immersion in the words and gestures of the character. When at last the makeup and costume are donned, the transformation is complete. The actor has stepped into the role, and as that being he steps into the reality of the character. Until that time a wig is nothing more than an artificial hairpiece, a drawing room only a stage set.

The tools used in a ritual are just props until they are changed into vehicles for transformation. A stick is not a wand, a table is not an altar, a glass of wine is not a chalice of nectar until you make them so. Your tools can likewise become power objects. They achieve this alchemy by carrying the energy of your intention, being specially crafted and/or consecrated, and by being cared for as if they were symbols of the sacred. A tool can be made or found. When you craft a tool, which may also be called a fetish or talisman, it holds the essence of what it is made from, the essence of who fashions it, and the essence of what it represents.

When a tool has become a symbol of power, you may want to use it in most or all of your rituals. A power object that represents some important aspect of your self or your growth can serve as a catalyst to connect you with that energy. You might choose to intensify this connection by creating a kind of permanent altar (a spot on a mantel or shelf) where you can set up the things that have particular meaning. That way you can have a brief personal ritual just by lighting a candle and being with the energy of the things on your altar.

Power objects are a natural lead-in to rituals. Even the acquisition of these items can be a ritual, or ritual-like. You might already have certain things that would be appropriate to symbolize the different Elements. A leisurely day at a secluded beach may have yielded a collection of shells, rocks, driftwood, and feathers. You carried these thing home and found a way to display them. Looking at them or holding them brings you back to that day, including your thoughts and feelings about it. These treasures already have the power of being able to elicit those pleasant memories; as vehicles capable of bringing on a shift in awareness, they are good options for ritual tools. These things can be used alone as they are, or creatively combined to symbolize the mingling of Water, Earth, and Air.

CRAFTING TOOLS

More power can be brought forth from these objects by crafting them into fetishes that combine other compatible things which hold the meaning of each Element for you. Here's an example: As I sit here writing this chapter, I find my thoughts are cloudy and lack focus. I decide to make a power object to assist in the unfettered flow of ideas whose goal expresses a particular concept. I decide to make something that ties together Air and Earth. The gift of feathers from a friend's macaw will represent Air, red linen thread (red for Fire) will be used for binding, and I will model a bird at rest out of bread dough. Bread exemplifies Earth. There will be holes poked in the dough for the thread to fit through. When the bird is baked and dry, it will be painted blue for clarity. I will wrap four groups of feathers, three feathers each, into bundles. In numerology, four is the number of the square and Earth, and three is the number of giving form to creative expression. In binding the feathers with the thread, I will bind in the intention with each wrap. Then I will tie each cluster to the bird. After the fetish has been blessed, I will place it above my desk.

The recipe for bread sculpture dough is: 4 cups of flour, 1 cup of salt, 1½ cups of water. Mix and knead the ingredients, adding more water if necessary. After shaping, bake at 300 degrees Fahrenheit for one hour. Paint and shellac.

A power object can have a special purpose, or it may hold the function of a ritual tool that is repeatedly used. If your rituals are likely to include a central altar or four directional altars, you may want to have permanent ritual tools to represent each of the Elements. These tools can be used for invoking (calling forth) the energy described by each Element, or for evoking the energy (calling it from within). Some of the more commonly used symbols lead the Tarot suits: cups or chalices represent Water, discs or pentacles are Earth, knives or swords represent Air, and wands express the energy of Fire. These things can be bought or in some way fashioned, cleansed, and blessed.

The Element Selection Guide at the end of Chapter 6 can give you some ideas of objects, actions, colors, and sounds that exemplify each of the Elements. Certain thing may "speak" to you, and these are the things you should consider for your tools. The intention for a ritual might give you ideas about power objects you would like to bring to that ceremony in addition to the Elemental tools. Making power objects may remind you of the projects you created in your first years of school. And indeed, the ideas and instructions for crafts in children's magazines and books are very suitable for this purpose.

Many of the items children use for art projects will be just what you need. Construction paper, chalk, paint, beads, buttons, seeds, oatmeal boxes, spools—the list should start unreeling from your early memory by now—will all be useful. Let's start with the materials for masks. A mask is a compelling vehicle for transfor-

"The only domain where the divine is visible is that of art, whatever name we choose to call it."

—*André Malraux*
Les Métamorphoses des dieux

mation. It can be simply made with paper bags, paper plates, or construction paper. The way the mask will be used should partially determine its composition.

A mask that is to represent a part of you that you wish to release or transform, such as your anger or fear, can be made from paper so that you can burn, tear, bury, or soak it. However, if you want your mask to connect you with the expression of an energy larger than yourself, it can be made more substantial and elaborate. A plaster mask can be decorated with paint, beads, feathers, sequins—almost anything that can be glued on. There are several kinds of plaster masks, but the following is quite easy and lots of fun.

Instructions for a plaster mask: Medical supply stores carry rolls of Specialist fast-setting plaster bandage. Buy several rolls to be sure you have enough. You will also need a place to lie down, some newspaper or towels to protect the floor and your clothing, a basin of warm water, scissors, a jar of petroleum jelly, and a friend. Pull back your hair and cover your face with a thin layer of jelly. Cut the bandage into strips about one inch wide and three inches long. Lie on your back, and have your friend dip the plaster strips into the water, press out any excess water, and then place the strips on your face, making a circle from hairline to ears. Don't go over your nostrils, or too far under your chin. You can have any size or shape eye openings and mouth opening, or if you prefer, your eyes and mouth can be closed and covered. The tape should be built about four layers thick, especially around the edges.

After a few minutes you will feel the first layers hardening and shrinking. When your friend has finished, you need to give the tape a few minutes more to harden sufficiently. Then, by wiggling your face, the mask will come loose. After you remove the mask, you can build up any areas you like with extra tape. Let it dry thoroughly before you attempt to decorate it.

When one puts on a mask, not only is there a transformation of outward appearance, but, on a more profound level, one's personality or character actually seems to be changed as well. There

is a kind of metamorphosis that occurs in which the inner, often unconscious, or archetypal elements of one's nature are brought forth and allowed expression.

The archetypes have many forms. It's almost as if your inner world were peopled with many different and sometimes incompatible figures. When you hold center stage, you may find yourself uncontrollably acting like an unruly child or a challenged warrior. At other times you may be expressing the seeker, or the wise old one. There are many ways besides mask-making to work with the archetypes in ritual. In most religions there are altars with statues representing some form of the Great Spirit.

You can create an image of a god or goddess, a power animal, or some aspect of your Self. A wire figure can be molded, painted, and dressed to achieve a good likeness.

Wire figures: The supplies you will need are: 14-gauge wire, picture wire, steel wool, a package of mache mix, acrylic or oil paints and a brush, pliers, and a wire cutter. Twist, cut, and wrap the 14-gauge wire into the skeletal form. Use the steel wool to create a musculature, and bind it to the skeleton with the picture wire. Mix the mache to the consistency of modeling clay, and cover the steel wool with it. You can mold or sculpt it for detailing. When the mache is dry it can be painted. You can make garments with paper or cloth and some glue. When you create a figure that comes from your unconscious, don't be surprised if the creation takes on a life of its own.

The energy of our unconscious can be accessed and channeled in other, equally effective ways. One of these is through dreams. Dreamwork, a ritualized way of communicating in the symbolic language of the unconscious, has been practiced from ancient through modern times. Dreams have many levels of expression. The mythic motif connects us with the collective unconscious. Our personal symbols provide doorways into the individual unconscious. Figures and scenes from waking reality can also be seen as symbols that mirror what is likewise a part of our inner world. As the Senoi people of Malaysia use their dreams to guide them in their outer life, so can we learn to understand and rely on the wisdom of our dreams.

Some dreams have enough impact to provide the outline for a ritual. Figures or symbols from your dreams can be brought into ritual as your personal gifts. Not everyone recalls their dreams at first. Recording dreams and impressions from the night when you wake up each morning will help in dream recall. A ritualized means to assist in remembering your dreams is by using a dream pillow. One of the properties of the herb mugwort is to aid in dream recall. A cup of tea made from mugwort can be drunk before bed each night, or you can make a small pillow and fill it with the dried herb.

Dream pillows: To make a pillow, you will need a piece of material about twelve inches long and six inches wide. Choose a color that you associate with night and dreaming. Black and silver are good choices. Collect things for decorations like crystals, moon shapes, ribbons, beads, or things symbolizing the kinds of dreams you'd like to have. You'll need an ounce or two of dried mugwort and any aromatic herbs you'd like. If you wish to find insight into your relationship issues, you can add dried rose petals or buds. Martial herbs like ginger or nettle can be added if you are looking for dreams to speak of your assertiveness or aggressiveness.

Bind, glue, or stitch any decorations onto the outside of the material. Fold it in half inside out, and sew up the sides and most of the top, leaving a hole about an inch and a half wide at the corner. Turn the bag to the right side through the hole and fill the bag with the herbs. Stitch the hole shut.

After the bag is blessed and consecrated, you can place it on your pillow. Before you go to sleep each night, hold the bag for a few minutes while you meditate on remembering your dreams. Sleep with the bag near your head.

> ***Herbal Incense:*** Dried herbs are known to have medicinal properties. Chamomile is relaxing and soothing. Peppermint soothes your stomach as well as clearing your head. Herbs can be taken internally or used in other ways. Herbs, roots, gums, oils, and resins are used in making incense. You can make your own by mixing the dried ingredients with a mortar and pestle and moistening them very slightly with oil. As you grind, mentally add the intention you wish the incense smoke to carry. Much easier than making your own incense is buying a roll of charcoals and burning the herbs and flowers on one of the discs.

The smoke from the burning incense bestows a cleansing or healing as it fills the air around you and within you. There must be a change on both an inner and an outer level for healing to occur. Sometimes change takes place within and is grounded through outward expression, other times the outer will resonate inward. This is one of the reasons we use the act of eating in ritual. It is a way to symbolically take something in and make it a part of you. When the incorporation of some quality is the purpose of your ritual, you can enhance this by modeling a power object representing that state out of something edible. A sweet choice is marzipan.

> ***Modeled marzipan:*** You can make marzipan by mixing ground almonds, egg white, and sugar, or you can purchase a tube of almond paste and follow the recipe on the label. Food coloring can be added if you like. Mold or sculpt any object you wish, or you can make a bowl that can be used to hold other ritual foods. When the piece is dry, glaze it with diluted egg white.

It seems that candles have a place in every ritual. If you make them yourself, they have even more meaning. Sand candles are easily molded in a bucket of tightly packed damp sand.

Sand candles: You will need beeswax sheets or paraffin wax, dye discs or wax crayons, wick (thin wick for thin candles, thick wick for thick candles), a sugar thermometer, and an old pan or double boiler. The wax should be carefully heated to 200 degrees Farenheit in a double boiler or in a pan that can float in another pan of water. If there is a fire, extinguish it by smothering it with the lid from a pot. Sculpt the shape you want for your candle in the damp sand. Pour the wax into the impression. When the wax has hardened, bore a hole for the insertion of the wick, and remove the candle from the bucket. You can seal the wick to the bottom of the candle with a bit of glue.

Of course, sand candles will not be suitable for all ritual purposes. You might find dipped candles to have a wider range of uses.

Dipped candles: Use the same materials and instructions listed above for sand candles. The wax need be heated to only 175 degrees Farenheit. You will need a deep container and a long wick. Pour the melted wax into the container. Fasten one end of the wick to a pencil and dip the free end into the wax. Take it out, let it harden, then dip it again. Repeat this procedure until the candle is as fat as you want it. You may need to reheat the wax from time to time. Dipped candles are often made in pairs, one wick dipped at both ends. When the candles are dried, they can be carved.

Candles may be used to symbolize illumination, but light or clarity can also be represented in other ways. Many of you may remember the wicked stepmother in the story of Snow-white. Each day she would gaze into her magic looking-glass and chant, "Looking-glass upon the wall, who is fairest of us all?" And the mirror would reply.

Mirrors symbolize truth, the reflection of divine wisdom. In rituals they can be used for skrying. When one mentally holds a question while gazing intently and single-mindedly into water, a crystal ball, or a mirror, a powerful form of symbol immersion is taking place. This concentrated involvement with a symbol can unleash its many meanings.

As a ritual object, a mirror has the power of representing all of the Elements: Air—vision, Fire—insight and illumination, Essence—seeing, as in coming to consciousness, Water—reflection, and Earth—the vehicle that contains these qualities. Bettye Edwards, in *Drawing on the Artist Within,* explores the concepts of illumination, intuition, and insight. She states:

> The root of *intuition* is *intuitus* . . . [from] the Latin verb *intueri,* to look at, and the word is defined as "the power or faculty of attaining direct knowledge or cognition without rational thought and inferences"—seeing something directly, or, in other words, "getting the picture," without having to figure it out. . . . A partner to intuition, *insight,* paradoxically refers directly to seeing and vision but means seeing something not necessarily visible, such as "seeing into" something, or "apprehending" something.[18]

> ***Magic Mirrors:*** A magic mirror can be made simply by gluing black felt to the back of a hand mirror, consecrating the mirror, and keeping it wrapped in black silk.

Consecration

Now that you have some ideas about how to make power objects to use in your rituals, you're ready to move on to the next stage of tool preparation—consecration. To consecrate a tool means to make it sacred. Some of the objects you choose to use in your rituals may already be sacred. A spiritual or religious statue or icon kept in a place of honor can certainly be an expression of the sacred. Yet you may find that the process of cleansing it allows its inherent quality to be even more present.

A complete cleansing involves the use of all five Elements, although very effective work can be done using the expression of a single Element. I remember being mystified as a child when my mother would ceremoniously bury something in the backyard to cleanse it. In my mind there was no way something would become clean by lying in the dirt for two weeks. Unfortunately my mother was unfamiliar with the principles underlying her actions. She could not explain that by burying something in the earth, or returning it to the Mother, it would be neutralized and born as if new.

In a five-Element cleansing, you can use Earth, preferably the purified type that is sold as potting soil, or salt crystals. For the Element of Water, boiled or bottled water can be used. Air cleansings are commonly done by smudging, the passing of burning incense or herbs. To cleanse with Fire means to pass the object through a flame, or for things for which this would not be suitable, a rose can be touched to them instead. The Element of Essence is most easily represented by the sun.

Ideally, every Elemental representation should first be cleansed by Essence. This means putting the salt, incense, and rose or candle on separate plates (preferably glass), the water in a carafe, and then placing all of these things in a safe, somewhat secluded spot where they can bathe in the sun's light. Ask that the rays of the sun purify these things as they are enveloped with Essential energy.

After a few hours you can remove the Elemental tools from the sunlight. Take the plate of salt, touch your hand to it and state: "May this salt be blessed with love and light. May all things negative be gone, and may only that which is good be held within." You can do the appropriate version of the same blessing for each of the other Elemental objects. When you have finished, the Elemental symbols will be ready to use in a ritual or to consecrate your tools.

For consecration, tools can be sprinkled with water, sprinkled with or touched to salt, passed through the flame of the candle or be touched with the rose, encircled with the smoke of the burning incense, and held up toward the sun. This process is similar to the consecration done during a ritual. When you are creating the ritual space, the cleansing can be done by walking around the space with the burning incense and with the lit candle, sprinkling the space with a mixture of the salt and the water, and imagining the sun filling and surrounding the area. When you are circling the space with the Elements, it is good to walk sunwise (clockwise), which creates energy. Counterclockwise movements break energy down.

The same process can be done for each of the ritual participants, as well as for the altar items. In doing consecrations, the cleansing may be all or just part of the procedure. A blessing can be included with the cleansing to fill the ritual space, objects, and members with their own Essential energy, after they have been cleansed of whatever was interfering or outmoded. Some blessings have the cleansing built in, and some cleansings include a blessing.

A blessing is a gift from the heart. Songs, poems, or chants that touch your heart can be adapted to your needs. There is a Native American chant I learned from Joan Halifax that makes a beautiful blessing: "Oh Great Spirit, Earth, Sun, Sky, and Sea: You are inside and all around me." As you speak or sing this chant, visualizing its message provides the blessing and cleansing.

Visualization is an excellent form of cleansing. Using color energy, you imagine a clear cloud or beam of the color passing through yourself or your tools. The color will wash away whatever needs to be cleansed. You then imagine that the chosen color remains, filling and surrounding you or your tools with its energy. Here are some traditional meanings associated with the colors. You may wish to "try on" various colors to discover what feelings they evoke for you.

COLOR CHART

Black—*silence and the mysteries*
Brown—*the earth; solidity, stability*
Purple—*religious dogma*
Lavender—*spiritual energy*
Navy blue—*institutionalized thought*
Sky blue—*clarity*
Turquoise blue—*insight*
Green—*growth*
Yellow—*warmth*
Orange—*vitality*
Red—*passion*
Silver—*lunar power*
Gold—*solar power*
White—*safety, protection*

You can charge a glass of water by mentally filling it with a color. You can then use the water for dipping, sprinkling, or drinking. Another way to charge water is by making a sun tea with stones. Sun teas are generally herbs placed into a jar of water and left in the sun. Stones and gemstones have healing properties as well. Emeralds are used for directing passions, rose quartz to bring peace to your heart, amethyst for balance and forgiveness, and opals to improve intuition. Lapidary shops sell not only the stones, but books explaining the correspondences.

Most of the items in this chapter can be found at craft shops, art supply stores, medical suppliers, or in nature. Never let the lack of the exact ingredient prevent you from making a tool. Even the things you have around the house can be used if they are properly cleansed and then treated as if they were no longer ordinary objects.

18. Bettye Edwards, *Drawing on the Artist Within* (New York: Simon & Schuster, Inc., 1986), p. 39.

Chapter 8

Altars

A n altar provides a symbol of the integrated wholeness of the Self and of the universe. It is the pivotal center point of balanced energies for your circle, for your consciousness. The word "altar" derives from the latin *altare,* a high place, and the use of high grounds as places of worship has been common to many cultures throughout human history.

Elevation allows you to see your surroundings; given the right weather, standing on high ground allows you to see the circle of the horizon around you as the central point—the image of Spirit. High places also allow clearer access to viewing the heavens, to metaphorically entering other worlds or planes of consciousness, and to receiving the guiding light of Spirit from the stars above.

A person standing atop a high place becomes a central pillar, mediating between the earth and the heavens, the interface between Spirit and matter, an axis mundi, which conducts energies between the planes of existence. Standing at the center is also symbolic of the birth of the universe, the One point manifesting from the zero, the line manifesting from the point.

Creating an altar is, in essence, recreating the origin of existence, and each time you construct or change an altar you have access to reliving this vital myth.

"We must never forget that one of the essential functions of the myth is its provision of an opening into the Great Time, a periodic re-entry into Time primordial."
—Mircea Eliade
Myths, Dreams, and Mysteries

Making an Altar

Different cultures have different types of altars. Some people use high ground, some construct a mound of earth for an altar, while others spend much time and energy on ornate altars built to precise specifications. All altars have some common symbolism, which you can use in making your altars.

Height: As discussed above, elevation is important in symbolically raising consciousness to the level of the sacred. The height does not need to be extreme. In your home a small table, windowsill, or shelf will be fine. A mantelpiece not only has extra height, but also carries the symbolism of the inner fire of Spirit in the fireplace below.

Altar Surface or Altar Cloth: The surface of your altar represents the emergence of something out of nothing in the reenactment of the origination myth. When you begin to set up an altar, after allowing the elevation of the altar itself to raise your consciousness, imagine the top of the altar, or the placing of the altar cloth, to represent the emergence from the Void of a sense of limitlessness. The altar surface can be viewed as a kind of infinite canvas upon which Spirit creates its manifestations.

The Center: From this endless expanse of possibility arises a point in the Center, from which all else emanates. This point is the One that contains all, the One in which everything finds relationship and meaning. On your altar you may represent this One by the altar cloth, by a simple symbol in the center of the altar, or by a central white candle or a plain oil lamp. The candle or lamp holds the special meaning of the light of Spirit or Essence, the one unifying light, as well as the sense of the axis mundi, which signifies our striving toward balance between Spirit and matter.

The Elements: As the One has risen from limitless possibility, so do the four qualities of the Elements arise from the One. As you build your altar, you are recreating this primal myth of emergence, and as you place your Elemental symbols upon the altar, you are recreating time and space. Imagine each Elemental tool to issue from the Center, from the One, as you place it in its appropriate quadrant (see Chapter 6, Elements of Ritual).

Types and Uses of Altars

Altars can be simple or complex, temporary or permanent, consistent or changing. Below you will find five categories of uses for altars. These categories correspond with Essence and the four Elements.

Essence ☉

To honor and increase your relationship with Spirit, you may choose to design a simple altar, which includes elevation, the altar surface or an altar cloth, and a single candle as described earlier. If you tend to the altar daily, you are symbolically attending to the sacred within yourself and in your world. Taking a moment upon rising in the morning to light the candle—striking the match high in the air and bringing it down to the wick is a gesture that represents bringing the higher energies of Spirit into the world—and imagining the light filling you is a fine way to center yourself in Spirit for the day.

Initiation/Energy △

You may want to honor specific aspects of the sacred in yourself and in your life. An altar that includes the four Elements as well as Essence can help balance and align you with these energies. Another way to bring this balance more fully into your life is to make an altar for each Element and set them up in the corresponding directional areas of a room. These altars can be as simple as four different colored candles, or you can use Elemental tools in each of the quadrants. Any of the altars we describe here can be set up around a room or on a single altar; choose whichever is more useful for you. If you feel you need to expand your consciousness, multiple altars might work better than a single one whereas a single altar may help increase your focus and concentration.

Merging/Mind △

You can also create altars to manifest certain qualities of the sacred you feel you need. If, for example, you feel you have been too harsh on yourself or others, you might want to build an altar for increasing compassion in yourself.

To accomplish this, you might choose your Elemental symbols from aspects of Water, which can symbolize giving, forgiveness, and an ability to flow around obstacles. You could place a soft blue towel on top of your altar cloth to represent a sea of loving kindness, with a fan of appropriate colors in the east to symbolize gentleness of thought, and a votive candle in a blue glass candle holder in the south to represent the softening of too-hot energies. A delicate vase with blue and white flowers or a silver cup of water in the west can remind you to be tender in your emotions, that they may give rise to beauty, and a seashell in the north can help you ground your energies in a pleasing and sound manner.

Deepening/Feeling ▽

The cyclical events in your life can be honored with altars. Many people decorate their homes with seasonal bouquets or other adornments representative of the time of year. Consciously constructing an altar to celebrate the season will not only bring beauty to your house, but will help you deepen your relationship to nature, your humanity, and Spirit as well.

A mantlepiece altar to recognize the return of the light during the winter solstice can use traditional winter symbols to help you deepen your connection to your own inner light. A black, deep green, or burgundy cloth can represent both the Void from which the One arises and the darkness of the winter days, which give birth to the light in mid-December. This light of Spirit can be present in a tall, central oil lamp, with the Element of Fire represented by a candle on each side. You can use a black and a white candle to signify the polarities with which many of us struggle during the dark times of our lives, and which are brought into proper relationship by the higher light of Spirit; or you may choose to use the traditional colors of red and green. These colors, too, imply a dance toward balance, with the cleansing and burning qualities of Fire always seeking equilibrium with the verdant expansion of natural growth.

This theme of balance and equilibrium can also be shown in using gray ribbons to represent the smoothing of emotions for the Element of Water, with expression in sound taking form on your altar with jingle bells on the ribbon ends for Air. The plants of the season can be used for Earth, holly providing the idea of increasing form with its sharp edges and red berries, and mistletoe, which grows not on the ground but high up in trees, and with its softer shape, giving rise to the concept of expansion. Creating such an altar can help you align the imbalances in yourself and approach your inner light, as we all approach the returning light at the solstice.

Manifestation/Body ▽

The altars you create for your rituals can be focal points for raising and stirring the consciousness of the participants. While all
rituals contain the Elements, follow the same basic process, and
reenact an archetypal myth, each ritual is unique to its particular
time, place, and the individuals involved in it. The ritual altar will
reflect its singularity in your choice of Elemental symbols and
their relationships to each other.

Chapter 6, The Elements of Ritual, has given you guidelines
for personalizing symbols, and we hope that the following altar
ideas for each type of ritual will help you integrate that information as well as inspire you creatively.

BEGINNINGS

Altar for a Baby Naming Ritual

After much deliberation, the new parents chose to name
their baby girl Rose, because it was their flower during courtship
and because the rose symbolized perfection, love, and heartful-
ness. They designed the altar for Rose's naming ritual around the
significance of their love and hopes for her, and the beauty of the
flower for which she was to be named.

They used a beautiful baby blanket they had received as a gift
for an altar cloth, and adorned it with pink and white ribbons, the
colors being those of the baby roses that surrounded the central
candle, and which symbolized, to them, purity and heart. The
central candle was white and inscribed with Rose's full name,
with the intention that as it burned, their child might be filled

with and fueled by the light of Spirit. The Fire Element was represented on the altar by a stained glass night-light in the shape of a rose, another gift from a friend who wished the light of love to shine forth even in the dark times of the new baby's life. Rose's aunt had calligraphed an explanation of the choice and meaning of Rose's name. This was placed in the eastern quadrant of the altar, and would be saved for Rose to read when she was older. In the west was a bowl of rosewater, which had also been charged with the baby's birthstone, and a cloth with which to wipe her forehead, hands, and feet during the ritual. For the Element of Earth, the parents had acquired a small evergreen sapling and a trowel to use in planting it in a special spot in their backyard; in caring for the tree during Rose's life, they would be reminded of this ritual and would be symbolically attending to her soul.

MERGINGS

Altar For A Wedding Ritual

The bride and groom designed this altar together with their minister and friends. The ribbons woven together atop the white altar cloth were symbolic of the merging of their two separate lives into a new and larger life, which can bring even more beauty and creation to the world than each could separately. Black and white candles represented the receptive and the dynamic, which merge into the light of Spirit while retaining individuality. The marriage certificate and bells to be used in the ceremony were placed in the east, and an entwined candle to be used on their honeymoon was in the south. In the west, a glass of wine to be blessed with the wishes of a few of their friends and family stood ready to be drunk, and the wedding rings occupied the northern area of the altar, to be given in the ritual as a token of their love and commitment.

CYCLES

A New Year's Eve Altar

This altar is set up around a room, allowing space for a large number of people to walk from station to station. In the east, the station of Air holds a table with paper and pens for guests to write down those parts of themselves that are antiquated and which hold them back from entering the New Year fully attuned to their inner selves and the will of Spirit. These papers can be cast upon the fire burning in the fireplace in the south, after which the participants can move to the table in the western quadrant of the room, to further cleanse themselves with a drink of champagne or sparkling water. Canapes from the northern table can help them ground their resolutions for the coming year, and all can gather around the candle on the central table, donning party hats and using noisemakers to celebrate the inner and outer return of another year.

ENDINGS

Altar For A Ritual For Leaving Home

When it was time for Joanna to move away to college, the family decided to do an ending ritual for her and themselves and created an altar to send Joanna on her way with their blessings. Her parents and siblings spent time choosing photographs of their precious moments together, pictures which embodied the spirit of their family. They placed them around a candle holder, which occupied the center of the altar. To express their support of continued communication with their daughter, the parents placed stamps and a long-distance telephone card in the quadrant for Air. Together the family had selected a garnet pendant for Joanna, which they placed in the south, representing both Joanna's personal energy and the energetic family support they desired to send with her as she entered her new life. Her younger sister placed the gift of a bottle of Joanna's favorite bubble bath in the west, so that Joanna could find emotional comfort in a warm bath and the love of her sister, as her sister had so often found solace in the care of her elder sibling. The seven-year-old brother made fudge, which he cut into big cubes and placed in a box in the north, to let Joanna know he thought she was sweet and so that she could have some nourishment from him on her trip.

Joanna was pleased with the gifts, deeply touched by the ritual, and surprised because she had planned one of her own for the family. When her ritual was complete, the altar contained her gifts to the family: in the east, a letter to the family, thanking them for what she had learned and how she had grown from

being in a relationship with each of the family members and with the family as a group; a homemade candle in the south, symbolizing how they had helped her find her inner light; a tape of her playing guitar and singing the family's favorite songs in the west; and a ceramic bowl filled with cookies especially baked with love in the north. Spirit was represented in the center of the altar by a picture she had painted.

HEALINGS

An Altar For A Ritual For Rest And Relaxation

Thomas was overworked and overextended; he had been having difficulty sleeping and was just plain exhausted. He developed a plan to keep his commitments within reasonable limits and a nightly ritual to help heal his exhaustion. He set up an altar on his night table to help him release his concerns of the day, center into himself, and receive the nourishment of Spirit while he slept. He would light the oil lamp in the center of the altar to invoke Spirit, and from that flame light a stick of his favorite incense to lift away his concerns for the night. He wrote in his journal while he sipped warm milk flavored with vanilla, and gazed at a lovely piece of rose quartz in the light of the lamp before going to sleep.

Chapter 9

Ritual Guidelines and Worksheet

In the four previous chapters, you received all the basic information needed to create your own rituals. This chapter will assist you in integrating, in a simple manner, the information and techniques from those chapters. By utilizing what you have learned, and following the guidelines and worksheet presented

TEN GUIDELINES FOR CREATING YOUR OWN RITUALS

1. Remember the intention.

2. Let the myth inspire you.

3. Use your intuition.

4. A ritual should benefit all and harm none.

5. Keep it simple.

6. Stay balanced.

7. Keep in touch with your feelings and with the other people.

8. Honor the power of words.

9. Keep the imagination alive.

10. Attend to detail.

here, you should be able to create a balanced, empowering ritual for any occasion.

The guidelines are simple but important. The worksheet corresponds to the Process Planning Guide in Chapter 5, The Process of Ritual, and can be used in each ritual you create.

1. *Remember the intention.*

In both the creation and performance of a ritual, the intention is the guiding force; without its presence, a ritual becomes a shell of what it can be. If at any point in the process—preparation, manifestation, or grounding—you find yourself worried, confused, or aggravated, you have lost touch with the intention. Focus your thoughts on the intention, or take a few breaths to release the distractions, and speak the intention silently or aloud until you are back in sync with it.

2. *Let the myth inspire you.*

You do not need to feel that you must formulate or enact a ritual merely on the strengths of your personal mind, desires, and talents. A ritual admits you to sacred time and space, into the archetypal realm of myth and mystery. You might choose to research myths and fairy tales with the same theme as the ritual you are planning, or explore how other cultures have realized intentions similar to yours. Allow yourself to be touched by our ancestral wisdom and the guidance of Spirit.

3. *Use your intuition.*

"The more we attempt to penetrate the secrets of Life, the deeper we become lost in its Mystery."

—William G. Gray
Ladder of Lights

Sometimes the inspiration of myth can give you so many ideas you don't know what to do with them. Allow your inner sense of the intention, and of what is appropriate, to help you to contain and provide form for your ideas. Imagine what the ritual can be like, and after thinking about what you can do, sit quietly, holding in your mind the plans you have made. Allow yourself to become aware of how this ritual would feel when enacted: Is it right for your purpose? Do you understand the meaning of the Elements you have chosen, and are they appropriate? Give equal time to intellect and intuition in planning a ritual, and it will be balanced and powerful.

4. *A ritual should benefit all and harm none.*

Participation in a ritual allows entry to mythic dimensions, from which we can increase both our consciousness and relatedness to ourselves, each other, our world, and Spirit. Any ritual that bears malice will reduce, if not destroy, the potential for healing that ritual holds. Malice affects not only the person at whom it is aimed, but the person who generates it as well.

5. *Keep it simple.*

It is easy to get carried away with the grandeur of myth when formulating rituals. Remember, however, that simple rituals are easier for most people to follow, and that focusing on a few symbolic acts provides a better avenue for entry into mythic consciousness than does a ritual cluttered with symbols and stories. The ritual should be short enough to hold the attention of all present, so omit all that is not really needed.

6. *Stay balanced.*

As we discussed in Chapter 6, The Elements of Ritual, balancing the actions and objects that represent the different aspects of yourself and the world is important. Throughout the various stages of creating your rituals, keep track of when you get off balance: worrying over details, getting washed over with intense feelings, letting pride interfere with the intention. Allow the balance you are creating in the ritual to remind you of the center in yourself, and allow your inner balance to flow into the ritual. Following the rhythms of your breath, and attending to the intention are two simple ways of returning to your center.

7. *Keep in touch with your feelings and with the other people.*

Increasing relationship is an important function of ritual, and so throughout the process attend to your feelings about yourself, the work, and the quality of connection among the participants. The more easily and smoothly feelings and ideas can be communicated during the preparation stage, the more you and the others will be open to the power and motion of the ritual in manifestation.

8. *Honor the power of words.*

What is spoken during a ritual has a much greater impact than if spoken in normal space-time. Because of this, choose what will be said and how it will be expressed with great care. While it is fine for some rituals to provide space for participants to speak from their hearts, for the most part there should be little extemporaneous speaking. Select poems or write words that mean exactly what you wish to convey, and practice delivering them for the best possible effect.

9. *Keep the imagination alive.*

We enter myth through the vitality of imagination. The symbology of a ritual should be a means to tap into the participants' unconscious. The simplicity of a ritual should allow their imaginations to create the consciousness of the myth that is being enacted. There is an easily recognizable vibrancy and regeneration that occurs when this consciousness is present.

10. *Attend to details.*

Every object and action in a ritual is there to help us alter consciousness in a specific way that honors the intention of the ritual. If you attend to the details, the impact of the ritual will be much greater, as you will be bringing the quality of the sacred into each particular aspect of the work. Rehearsals are of great benefit in helping you set the proper tone, regulating the timing of actions, and reducing performance anxiety so that your attention during the ritual itself can focus on the ritual intention. Even if a full rehearsal is not possible, practicing your actions and what you will say will help. Everything you do in a ritual has symbolic meaning and impact, so attend to the details.

In Chapter 5, we presented the Process Planning Guide, which led you through planning, manifesting and grounding a ritual. The following Ritual Worksheet expands on the Process Planning Guide, integrates the information on Elements and symbol selection from Chapter 6, and provides you with space to write in all the details needed at each stage of your ritual.

To help you better understand how a ritual works, each stage and each section is marked with its Elemental symbol: △ Fire, △ Air, ▽ Water, ▽ Earth, or ⊙ Essence. For a ritual to have symmetry, it follows the stages of inspiration △, creation △, formation or deepening ▽, and action or manifestation ▽, as does any creative process. In astronomical theory, the stars were born from the condensation of the primal, or "essential" matter of the universe. The fiery masses that are stars produced gases which, as they cooled, further condensed into liquids and then solids. Looking at this process in terms of the Elements, we see that Essence gives rise to Fire, from which issue increasingly "denser" manifestations of being: Air, to Water, to Earth. These stages of the development of the universe are analogous to those of a ritual.

Within each of these stages the four Elements are also present in energy △, mind △, feeling ▽, and objects or actions ▽. These stages and Elements were discussed in the last two chapters. By using this worksheet you will gain more understanding of their relationships to each other and of their interactions within a ritual.

In the preparation stage, you will notice that the stages flow downward from inspiration to action, into the beginning stages of the manifestation of the ritual. There the movement is from Earth back up toward Fire, and Essence, at the invocation and direction of higher energies. These energies are then brought down through the Elements from Fire to Earth again in the closure of the ritual. The grounding phase again brings the flow from Earth to Fire, making a complete round of the Elements—from Fire (inspiration for the ritual) to Earth (physical preparation/creating sacred space) to Fire (invocation) to Earth (ritual closure/breakdown of sacred space) to Fire (integration). The central point of this cycle is Spirit or Essence, and the beginning and the ending are inspiration. So, too, is it with existence (you will find a basic outline of this process in the Conclusion).

While you may not need to use the worksheet for simple rituals, you may find it essential in organizing more complex ones. We recommend working with it a few times, until you have integrated all aspects of creating rituals and feel comfortable without the worksheet. Even then, it can serve as a useful guideline.

RITUAL WORKSHEET

I. PREPARATION/CREATION

△ A. CLARIFYING THE INTENTION
(Inspiration)

△ 1. What is the inspiration for this ritual?

△ 2. What myth does it reenact? What type of ritual is it?

▽ 3. What effect do you want this ritual to have, and on whom?

▽ 4. Clearly state the intention of this ritual:

△ B. PLANNING (Creation)

△ 1. What symbols are you using in this ritual?

Fire _____

Air _____

Water _____

Earth _____

Essence _____

△ 2. Write out a draft of the ritual itself, using the Process Planning Guide and the Manifestation section below for guides.

▽ 3. Logistics: Write out dates, times, deadlines, what needs coordination, and who needs to be contacted.

▽ 4. Make a shopping list of materials you need.

▽ C. EMOTIONAL PROCESS (Deepening)

△ 1. What feelings or issues have been brought up by the preparation you've done so far?

△ 2. Have any ethical questions arisen? Is there any way this ritual could hold negative intention for anyone?

How?

▽ 3. What other limitations (money, space, time) have you encountered?

▽ 4. Working through those feelings, ethical issues, and limitations, what adjustments, if any, need to be made to your ritual plan?

▽ D. PHYSICAL PREPARATION (Action)

△ 1. What else needs to be coordinated?

△ 2. What materials need to be gathered?

▽ 3. Details for arriving with helpers and checking that you have everything you need:

▽ 4. Cleaning the physical space: What needs to be done, when, and by whom?

II. *MANIFESTATION: THE RITUAL ITSELF*

▽ A. CREATING SACRED SPACE (Action)

▽ 1. What objects and actions will you use to clear and bless the space?

▽ 2. What emotions do you need to clear from yourself? How will you do this?

△ 3. How will you center yourself?

△ 4. How will you ask for guidance in conducting this ritual?

Using the circle below, write in how you will set up the temple/sacred space, including location of your chosen symbols, where participants will enter and stand, and other appropriate details.

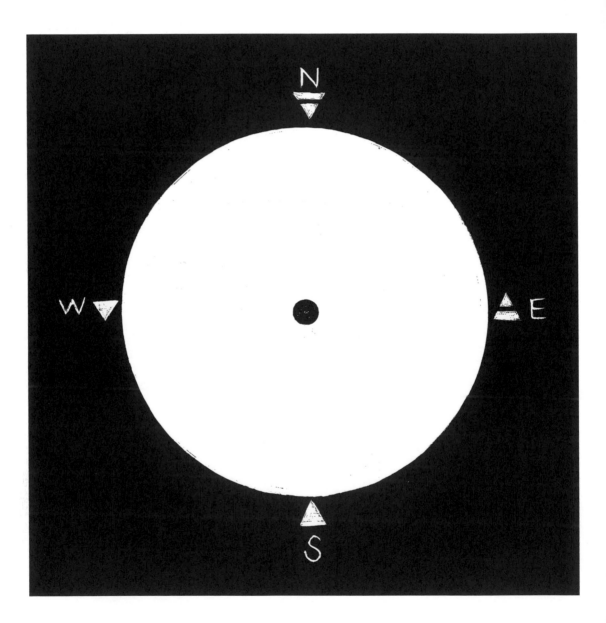

B. SETTING THE MOOD (Deepening ▽), and DECLARATION OF INTENTION (Creation △)

▽ 1. What objects and actions will you use?

▽ 2. Music, sounds:

△ 3. Poetry and speech:

△ 4. What will these things inspire in the participants?

⊙ C. INVOCATION (Inspiration △) and DIRECTION OF HIGHER ENERGIES (Creation △)

△ 1. What particular energies are you invoking, and precisely what do you want them to do?

△ 2. What words will you use to direct these energies to their purpose?

▽ 3. What emotions will be touched, and what kinds of rhythms or music will help you accomplish this?

▽ 4. What objects and actions will best represent and channel these energies and the emotions of the participants?

D. BLESSING (Deepening ▽) and CLOSURE (Action ▽)

△ 1. With what gift of Spirit will the participants leave the ritual?

△ 2. Words or poetry you can use to name this gift:

▽ 3. Music and sounds to enhance the gift and mark the ending of the ritual:

▽ 4. Actions and objects used to mark the ending. How will the participants leave the sacred space?

III. *GROUNDING/COMPLETION*

▽ A. BREAKDOWN OF SACRED SPACE (Action)

△ 1. What is left to be done (blessed food or drink needing proper disposal, for example)?

△ 2. How will you release the sacred space back to normal space?

▽ 3. Emotional completion: How will you give thanks?

▽ 4. When will you break down the circle, put things away, and clean up? Who will help?

▽ B. EMOTIONAL PROCESS (Deepening)

▽ 1. Did you experience any strong physical sensations during the ritual?

▽ 2. What emotions were raised?

△ 3. What did you learn about yourself?

△ 4. How does your emotional experience relate to the myth enacted in the ritual?

△ C. EVALUATION (Creation)

▽ 1. What worked and didn't work effectively?

▽ 2. How impactful was the ritual to those involved?

△ 3. If you were to do this ritual again, how would you improve it?

△ 4. What new ideas or insights did you gain about the nature of ritual?

△ D. INTEGRATION (Inspiration)

△ 1. How were you inspired by this ritual?

△ 2. How can you use this inspiration to create change in yourself?

▽ 3. What form do you imagine these changes can take in the world?

▽ 4. What actions can you take this week to manifest this inspiration?

Chapter 10

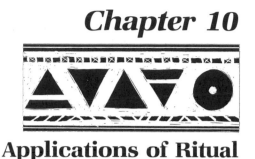

Applications of Ritual

Throughout this book we have given you numerous examples of the applications of ritual and helped you to see where ritual can be useful in your life. This chapter further explores ways that ritual can create balance and strength in your life as an individual and as a person in relationship with others.

We have divided this chapter into four sections: Individual Rituals; Rituals in Relationships; Family Rituals; and Group Rituals. In each section we approach the application of ritual from four different directions: the physical world of manifestation; the emotional world of deepening; the mental world of relatedness; and the spiritual world of initiation. These approaches correspond to the Elements of Earth, Water, Air, and Fire, which were discussed in Chapter 6 and have been a common theme throughout this book. Each section provides examples of rituals that will enable you to recognize and use ritual as a powerful tool in your life.

INDIVIDUAL RITUALS

The Physical World/Manifestation ▽

Rituals can be of great assistance in dealing with difficult transitions in the physical world. Such changes might include moving to another state, being put on a strict diet by your doctor, recognizing physical limitations, or turning a particular age. In Chapter 5, we describe a ritual for a fortieth birthday to help you deal with dread, self-doubt, and the approach of middle age. As well as using rituals to help cope with change, you can also create rituals to help you make changes in the physical world.

RITUAL TO QUIT SMOKING

After five years of smoking tobacco and three unsuccessful attempts at quitting, Ron decided a ritual was in order.

Preparation: On a brisk March day, carrying a knapsack with a canteen of water, an apple, journal and pen, matches, and his last two cigarettes, Ron hiked into the hills near his house. He traveled through parts of the woods he knew well, past the bog and into new territory. As he scrambled over some rocks, a strong wind greeted him, and the sun shone warmly on his face. Looking at the inspiring view all around, he decided that that was the spot.

Manifestation: It was a small, private outcropping of rock and soil on the northern side of the hill. He walked around the space and found a confortable place to sit and smoke his last cigarette. As he struck the match, he stated his *intention* that this would be the last cigarette he would ever need. While he smoked, he thought about all the times tobacco had been useful to him, how much he hated to give it up, and how it interfered with his life. He let his thoughts and feelings rise with the smoke.

Water from the canteen cleansed his mouth and throat and extinguished the cigarette, which he crumpled and buried in the dirt. He was, symbolically, quenching his need and burying his dependency. He stood, holding the other cigarette high, and asked aloud that the wind accept it as an offering, that Air assist him in not smoking. A gust of wind pulled the cigarette from his fingertips, and he inhaled the cold, clean air. He stated that whenever he needed to smoke, he would call upon the wind to help him abstain. He then ate the apple to ground that promise. He gave thanks to Spirit for the wind, the sun, the water, the earth, and the tool of ritual.

Grounding: He wrote down the experience in his journal. On the way home he buried the apple core at a place that seemed ready for an apple tree.

During the next few years, whenever he felt the desire for a smoke, he would breathe deeply, or, better yet, get a taste of the wind through a door or window. The fresh air filling his lungs, and the memory of the wind accepting his offering, was better than any cigarette could have been.

The Emotional World/Deepening ▽

You can use ritual to help you through difficult times. Dealing with depression is something that plagues us all now and then.

RITUAL TO RELIEVE DEPRESSION

We designed a ritual for a man who had been feeling depressed for several months after a job loss and was beginning to worry about himself.

Preparation: He was instructed to find a heavy overcoat and several layers of heavy clothing. On the overcoat he was to pin slips of paper that named his bad feelings, such as "hopeless," "useless," "worthless," "apathetic," and so on. He also was to come up with one thing he did not feel bad about in his life. This turned out to be playing with his child.

Manifestation: On the day of the ritual, he was to wake up, darken a room by drawing all the curtains, and don all the heavy clothing, topped with the overcoat. Then, for no less than thirty minutes, he was really to get into moping, dragging around, or lying moaning on the floor. He would pull one slip of paper from the coat at a time and get really involved with that feeling. When he'd gone through all the papers, he crumpled them up and burned them in a safe container, saying good-bye to each one. Then he took off the coat and all the clothes, opened the curtains, and went into the bathroom to shower, shave, and dress in something he really liked. When he was dressed he took his child to the zoo for the afternoon, and did not return until he was sure they'd both had a very good time.

Grounding: When they arrived back home, it was to a surprise dinner his wife had prepared. Attempting humor, she had made a dinner using mostly "light" foods. He later reported that his depression had lifted considerably.

The Mental World/Relatedness △

When you are working on a project and feel "stuck," ritual can help you move beyond it. Ritual can be used to help you open up to artistic inspiration or to clarify and deepen your creative process.

RITUAL TO PREPARE FOR WRITING

Preparation: In writing this book we used many rituals. To prepare myself for writing, I would first clean the room and gather my materials.

Manifestation: After lighting a candle, I would walk to the east side of the room and ask Air for clarity of thought. Moving clockwise, to the south I would ask Fire for the energy and inspiration necessary for the task. In the west, the request to Water was for smoothness and depth of feeling, and that I might be in touch with that which we all share. The north was the place to ask Earth for help getting my thoughts, feelings, and inspirations down on paper. After going to the east to complete the circle, I would return to center, where my writing chair is, and ask for guidance, that the book be written to further the Divine Will.

Grounding: I would give thanks and begin to write. This ritual helped me clear and focus myself. The writing that followed flowed much more easily—and needed fewer rewrites—than the work done without the ritual.

RITUAL TO IDENTIFY THE CAUSE OF AN OBSESSION

Rituals can also be used to deal with obsessions. A ritual was designed for Neil, who developed an obsession with his new car. He realized things had gotten out of hand when he found himself going down to the parking lot to inspect his car every lunch hour and then washing it every afternoon when he arrived home from work.

Preparation: He wasn't sure if it was the car itself that meant so much to him, or if there were some unknown feelings that were manifesting symbolically. We decided upon a ritual to help identify what was really going on. His ritual centered around a dialogue with the obsession.

Manifestation: At a selected time and place he prepared to invoke the essence of his obsession and imagine it come to life in a space a few feet before him. He treated this essence as if it were the genie that emerged from the bottle in the old fairy stories. He questioned it carefully and thoroughly and let the answers come to him. By the time he was finished, he had come to realize that the car was such a major investment that he was not sure he had a right to it. He had to be careful to keep it in perfect condition, as if he had surreptitiously acquired it and it might disappear or be taken away.

Grounding: With this realization, he was able to work with the connection between his image of himself and the symbol of the expensive new car and create more balance.

The Spiritual World/Initiation △

Some people find that ritual is a beneficial form of spiritual practice. Meditation, contemplation, and prayer are all forms of practice that can be useful to you at different times in your life, and you have probably found that one of these forms is more suited to your personal style than are the others. It is important in setting up a spiritual practice to work with a form that feels right to you and challenges you as well. If you are a deeply passionate person, for example, prayer may be second nature to you and the form you use most often. It would probably be useful for you to include a less emotional form of devotion in your practice as well, such as sitting meditation or contemplation, to help stir you out of imbedded personality patterns and create more balance in your life. Ritual can be useful in both of these endeavors.

Beth had been working on self-growth for several years and was anxious to incorporate new tools that would help her to be more consciously "on her path." One day after reading an article about the Goddess religion, she decided to look for ways to be more in harmony with the cycles of nature. She decided to create a ritual to do at each new and full moon. With the new moon symbolizing beginnings, she designed a ritual as a time for seeding plans for the month. In the full moon ritual she let herself discover and give thanks for whatever she had reaped that month. This included finding ways she had met and conquered challenges, as well as things that were obvious blessings.

Other people might prefer a daily practice. This could be as simple as lighting a candle and asking Spirit for balance in body, feeling, mind, and soul as you wait for the kettle to boil each morning. It is simple to do, and a fine way to start the day. More elaborate rituals—similar to the circle described earlier in this chapter in the ritual to prepare for writing—can certainly be used, but when beginning a practice, a ritual works best that is not too complex. Over time, the morning candle ritual brings much more balance into your life and increased awareness of Spirit throughout the day.

RITUALS IN RELATIONSHIPS

During your life you are in different important one-to-one relationships. You are a friend, a child, a lover, a parent, or perhaps a business partner. In this section we discuss how you can use ritual to honor and assist changes that occur in such relationships.

The Physical World/Manifestation ▽

We have cultural rituals for weddings, and we celebrate anniversaries, but we could also use ritual to honor a new partnership, or a deepening of commitment between friends. We can also use ritual to help resolve problems in relationships and strengthen our bonds.

A good relationship is built actively and over time. When two people get together, no matter how compatible they are, there will be important differences between them. Sometimes we assume we understand someone's behavior when we are only interpreting it through our own filters. Two business partners who had begun a new venture found themselves faced with misunderstandings of each other's actions and moods. They developed a ritual based on role reversal to help them understand how they each perceived the other. Using this theme, they agreed to spend an entire day in the emotional and behavioral role of the other, acting as they felt the other acted. Afterward they processed what came up for each of them, and found out that they were both sharing fears about their new venture they thought the other did not have. They were then able to get back in sync with each other and work effectively.

The Emotional World/Deepening ▽

ENDING RITUAL FOR A RELATIONSHIP

Tom and Jean decided to separate after being together for three years. Couples counseling had helped them recognize that they still loved each other, but that they had grown in different ways. Their old relationship no longer suited either of them, and to keep it up only led to fights and pain. They wanted to remain friends but did not know how to let go of their past way of relating. They decided to do a ritual.

Preparation: After planning and preparing, they drove to the country, riding around until they found an appropriate place.

Manifestation: They dug a hole and placed some artifacts of their relationship in it—a few gifts, a letter, a shared pillowcase. During the week, Tom had written a poem, and Jean had made a picture, symbolizing the significance of what they previously had together. They shared these creations with each other and discovered they had each included what they had hoped the relationship would become.

Together they put the drawing and poem into the hole and set them on fire. They acknowledged these symbols of their past and of their hopes and let their desires and their old form of relating pass away as the papers burned.

Grounding: When the fire was out, they covered it with dirt and planted flowers over the remains of their old relationship. As they watered the flowers, they said a prayer that what had died could find life in a new and better form. They then held each other and wept together, glad that they did not have to go through this ending alone.

A few months after this ritual took place, Jean and Tom found they were able to become friends, even though it was a bit awkward at first. Their relationship changed and grew, as did they.

The Mental World/Relatedness △

A pair of friends were both going through stressful periods in their lives, and found that when they got together, they often ended up commiserating with each other, rather than doing the creative projects that were so nourishing to them and their relationship. They chose to integrate a "worry box" into a healing ritual for themselves. They wrote each of their worries for themselves and their relationship on separate cards, including the reason for the concern, the worst fear, and how far inside or outside of their range of control the worry was. An example of this would be worrying about making a deadline versus whether or not there would be a major earthquake. They placed the cards in a box and designated certain times when they met to worry—the ten minutes after their first cup of coffee together. They worried as much as they could during the specified time, but when worries came up later in their conversation, they reminded themselves to wait until the next worry period and got involved with a project instead. They noticed that they often found solutions to their concerns at the end of the worry periods, and were able to come up with creative ways to implement those solutions.

The Spiritual World/Initiation △

A couple we know was very happy together. Their only area of contention was in recurrent arguments over religious matters. They were each very devoted spiritually, but to two significantly different paths. They devised a ritual to help them better understand the other's views and beliefs and to transcend the different forms of the Spirit from whence each form was created.

Preparation: Both took time to look more deeply at their chosen paths in terms of the archetypes of the Elements, the types of rituals used within their systems, and basic tenets of the path. Together they built an altar with symbols from both paths in each quadrant.

Manifestation: During the ritual they explained to each other the meaning of their symbols and their celebrations, noting how they were different from yet similar to each other. This led them to an exploration of the nature of Essence, and how each of their paths worked for them with their different styles of being in the world.

Grounding: They sat quietly and meditated upon what they had learned, not only about the other's system and self, but about their own path and person and the meaning and presence of Spirit. To ground this process they presented one another with gifts they had chosen within the other's symbolic system, as a gesture of support and understanding.

FAMILY RITUALS

Rituals come naturally to families. This section covers how to improve and deepen rituals that are already present in a family, as well as other applications of ritual in family life. Changing residences, buying a summer cottage or a new family car can be times for celebration and are times to honor change.

The Physical World/Manifestation ▽

Sue and Steven and eight-year-old Terry were moving into their new house! They wanted a ritual that would cleanse the feeling of previous tenants and welcome them into their new home, a place of nurturance, support, happiness, and growth. As a newly blended family, it was also important that the ritual generate energy for their family as a unit.

NEW HOUSE RITUAL

Preparation: A few friends gathered and enlisted Terry's aid in making candle holders from aluminum foil. We enjoyed his creations, and he helped us place one in each room.

Manifestation: We all gathered in the kitchen—the heart of the house. After stating our *intention* and the opening prayers, the eight adults set out. We took bells and drums, and burning sage, throughout the house and around the property, making quite a racket, to clear out the old energy. Terry thought we were all a bit loony and watched us with puzzled amusement. When we went through the house a second time, saying a blessing in each room, Terry joined us. His chosen task was to light each candle with a large wooden fireplace match.

Grounding: We ended the ritual with a wine blessing. Each guest poured wine into a cup as they expressed their wishes for Terry, Steve, and Sue. The family poured some of the wine onto the earth, to symbolize sharing their blessings, and drank the rest to "digest" the good wishes. The three of them placed the gift of a triple-joined crystal on the mantlepiece, in recognition of their unity. They had joined together and made the house truly theirs.

The Emotional World/Deepening ▽

Families support each member in dealing with individual difficulties, disappointments, and losses. Families also celebrate the success of the individual members be it getting a new job, being awarded a scholarship, or winning a race or a spelling bee.

To celebrate an important event in my family, we would make a toast using special blue-and-white glasses. My father was a glassblower and had made a personalized glass for each of us. The glasses were only used at very meaningful times, and the event was recorded on a paper kept with the glasses in their own box. The toast always preceded a specially cooked dinner which we would eat by candlelight in the warmth of our happiness and unity. A simple ritual, but one that touched us all deeply.

The Mental World/Relatedness △

Power struggles in a family can severely undermine the love and security we rely on families for. The Taylor family ran into trouble when a job transfer prompted a move to another city. The two children, aged twelve and fourteen, felt betrayed and manipulated and decided to fight back. The key to a successful ritual in this case was to create a situation in which the children could feel that their lives, including their wants and needs, were as important as those of their parents. To accomplish this, the children were permitted to plan a farewell party for friends of the entire family.

As each individual grows through life, families are affected by these passages. Ritual can help ease the transitions of starting school, reaching puberty, retirement, and menopause. The form of the family changes as well. There are births and adoptions, divorces, the blendings of two families in marriage, death of a family member or a family pet, children moving out, children growing up, and sons- and daughters-in-law to be welcomed. Rituals can be valuable in supporting all of these changes.

The Spiritual World/Initiation △

Anniversaries, birthdays, and holidays are examples of cyclical rituals in families. You can also create rituals for the single purpose of celebrating the love that exists in the family. Doing so honors and deepens the family bonds and each individual's sense of belonging.

FAMILY DINNER RITUAL

If you have Sunday family dinners, you could choose one Sunday a month for a ritual dinner. The Sunday closest to the new moon is a good time to sow the emotional and energetic seeds you would like to see grow and bloom in the coming month.

Preparation of the dinner can be a group endeavor, and special care can be taken in setting the table to inspire beauty, harmony, and union.

Manifestation: Before soup or salad, each person can thank each of the family members individually for something he or she has done in the past month that has benefited the family. Prior to the main course, each member can thank the others for personal qualities that they possess and that are appreciated. Before dessert, everyone can state something about themselves that they like. Following dessert, each person can name a quality of the family that is precious to them, that helps them in their life, and that they would like to receive more of in the coming month.

Grounding: In the coming month, each person can remember and act on the qualities named during the ritual. When such seeds are sown in love, they are sure to flourish.

GROUP RITUALS

Clubs, school classes, businesses, sports teams, and musical bands are some of the groups that can benefit from ritual. While these groups are formed for different purposes, they all move through some similar transitions, which are related to those discussed in the previous section on families.

Manifestation/Physical World ▽

Neighborhoods are no longer made up of families who have come to know each other over the years. On many blocks, there are so many units with people coming and going after only a short time that many neighbors do not even recognize each other. The crime rate in cities is increasing rapidly, so on some blocks, the residents have found home alert meetings to be useful. A representative from the police department comes to one of the homes where all the interested neighbors have gathered, and they discuss safety measures and agree to watch out for each other. This ritual-like situation can be enhanced by the neighbors having a kind of block party. In addition to socializing and discussing safety, they can also work on networking or creating a skill bank or job core. This can include babysitting, recycling, gardening, hauling, and other things that some neighbors may need and others may be able to provide.

The Emotional World/Deepening ▽

Group members can be supported in their individual transitions with group rituals as well. When a friend of ours was getting married, we gave her a ritual bridal shower. As part of the ritual, each of Donna's women friends brought a present representing a different aspect of being a woman. For the "little girl," Donna received a book of fairy tales and a jar of bubbles. She was given a negligee to honor the "temptress/lover" aspect of the feminine and a crystal pendant and a journal to keep her in touch with her "wise old woman." A golden paper crown celebrated the "queen of the realm" of the household and was followed by the gift of a pillow, on which the queen could rest her weary head after a day of toil. At the end of the ritual, we felt full and powerful. Donna was able to bring herself to her wedding day with the aspects of the feminine whole balanced within.

The Mental World/Relatedness △

Many groups are formed around creative projects. The alignment of a group for a specific purpose is in itself such a creative project, and many groups use ritualized behavior to gather and focus their energy.

Before a big football game, there are pep rallies and pep talks in the locker room. The team forms a circle to raise their energy and unite them before they charge onto the field. This ritual action might be made even more effective with the conscious intention of the team members doing their best, both individually and collectively, and focusing less on beating the other team.

A singing group entering a competition could use a ritual to help them align with each other and sing better than ever before. While this could involve a complex ritual, it could also be something as simple as the group forming a circle, holding hands, focusing their intention, and chanting "Om" together, as a means of aligning themselves while increasing their consciousness and skill.

The Spiritual World/Initiation △

As well as needing alignment to purpose, a group can be in need of healing. Whether it be poor communication, general grumblings of dissatisfaction, or a budget crisis, a group can benefit from dealing with its problems in the realm of Spirit as well as in the arena of practical problem-solving.

One way to approach this is to offer a healing circle at the end of community meetings once business has been attended to. Those who wish to participate can join in a circle and clear themselves from heavy concerns by concentrating on their breath, and filling themselves with light. By imagining the light of the individuals blending, participants can get in touch with their relationships with each other and with the group, and can also get a clearer sense of the community energy or group soul. Similar to the ritual for planetary healing in Chapter 4, the community members imagine the wounds of the group healing and ask the group soul or higher powers to fill the entire organization with light and wellness. This unites the community and enables Spirit to help smooth and guide the way through difficulties.

Chapter 11

The Rite of Spring

This chapter is composed of two complete rituals that were created to welcome spring and all that the season symbolically implies. The first ritual is one that can be done alone, or it can be the individual prelude to the second ritual, which is also in honor of spring, but designed for a group. Both the individual and group ritual follow the steps outlined in Chapter 5.

Feel free to use one or both of these rituals for yourself. You can follow them directly or modify them to suit your needs.

INTRODUCTION

Linda entered therapy with me, complaining of dissatisfaction in her relationships, guilt over outbursts of anger, and a pervasive sense of emptiness. A thirty-six-year-old woman from a lower-middle-class background, she sensed her life and her work were devoid of meaning. Emotionally she felt great pain, fear, and rage, but little joy. The hollowness she experienced led her to question whether or not she wanted to stay alive.

During the three years we worked together, we explored many different aspects of her life and her pain. She courageously descended into forgotten childhood memories to retrieve the little girl huddled, scared and shaking in dark terror. Gradually she came to understand the cause of her anger, and her tantrums subsided. She began to experience pleasure and some joy, and her scathing humor softened and lightened. By her thirty-ninth birthday she was feeling much better about who she was and her increased ability to choose how to act in the world. When she went inside herself, however, she still felt there was nothing but a hollow tube, void of light or life.

We spent many sessions exploring that void, searching for signs of something, of anything, and by winter Linda was ready to give up looking. "There's nothing there. We've looked and looked, and there's nothing there. Why bother to go in again? I'll get by fine on the outside, and just give up hoping for anything on the inside." Despondent, she went away for the winter holidays.

When we resumed our work in January, Linda reported a dream: She is searching and searching, lost in the void for years, drifting, a shell of nothing. At some point, isolation fills her, and she cries out to an unbelieved-in God for help, certain it is hopeless. She continues to drift in the emptiness. Then something catches her eye—a light, far off, distant, and dim. Her heart begins to race, and she awakens in fear, sweating, and trembling.

In our sessions throughout the winter months, we repeatedly went back to that light, working through her fear, getting closer to the light. Linda became filled with an incredible anticipation, which shone in her face. As spring approached, the light continued to grow, and Linda discovered that the light was a symbol of her sense of worth and meaning, which had been buried under an aeon of "nothingness" to survive the chaos and brutality of her early life. She felt *almost* ready to embrace the light as her Self, but needed some structure within which to do so, some way to bring the inner light into outer reality. I suggested a ritual, similar to the one presented in the following pages.

"At first I was skeptical," Linda confides. "We had done some symbolic work in therapy, but doing an actual ritual seemed a bit bizarre. Once I got involved with it though, it really helped me to embrace and nourish that inner light."

In the beginning stages of the "sprout ritual," Linda experienced heavy resistance, both to the ritual and to her inner movement. "I would be busy and forget to rinse and water the seeds sometimes; it helped me realize how much of my life had been occupied with distractions—with keeping my energy and attention away from my inner truth so that it would be safe. But now it *is* safe, and it's time for my true Self to come forward."

Linda completed the sprout ritual the day before the vernal equinox, and with her newly-embraced Self decided to join the spring group ritual we held the next day. This ritual was based on the one presented here, following the sprout ritual, and during it Linda received a sense of participation and mystery that was new to her. "It took a lot of courage for me to stand up with a bunch of other people and speak about my struggle and my growth, but the group was really supportive and accepting. The ritual I did alone allowed me to honor and accept my Self and get in touch with the depth of my relationship with nature. The group ritual

let me realize—after all that time spent in the void—that I was not alone, that there are other human beings who seek and search and struggle. I was also really moved by the larger presence that seemed to fill and work through the group. And now at times when I forget that I believe in myself, or I feel weak and alone, I can call on that presence. And it helps."

Ritual is a powerful tool for growth. Linda was able to use ritual to afford her a completion of her years of struggle and an initiation into a new way of being. Since the ritual, she is exploring new work opportunities, thinking about going back to school, and feeling ready for a new relationship. We meet in therapy about once a month, but her major work there is done. She is moving on, into a life no longer shadowed with emptiness and pain, but instead filled with light, strength, and relatedness. She is in touch with her vitality, and with the larger Spirit that guides and nourishes us all. While ritual is certainly not solely responsible for her metamorphosis, it was an important tool in her growth.

RITUAL FOR INDIVIDUAL EXPRESSION

Preparation. Begin by *clarifying your intention.* Step one: It is
spring, either by the calendar or by the weather. The changing of
the seasons offers an excellent opportunity for a cyclical celebration. In some of the traditions where ritual has a large role, such
as the shamanic or Wiccan ones, aligning your inner world with
the greater cycles of the earth is a powerful way to achieve both
inner balance and understanding of the rhythm of change.

What happens in the outer world, in nature, during spring?
This is the season when we see the gray, solemn mantle of winter
burst into life. Spring is the time of rebirth and new beginnings.
It holds a sense of possibility, hope, vitality, and release. Spring is
not only a cyclical celebration but also a beginning. In many ways
it is appropriate to think of spring, or the spring equinox, as the
beginning of the year.

If we take all the outer world associations for spring and reflect on them, we can then move on to step two in the planning
process. If you would like to perform a ritual for yourself, you
can focus on bringing yourself out from the constraints of winter.
This release needs time to take hold. For this ritual you will be
involved in a process that unfolds over four to seven days. Each
day there will be a few short periods of time spent with cleansing,
releasing, and reflecting. This will culminate in a ceremony that
will take about an hour. This sequence, which will lead you
through a gradual awakening, is much like the transformation
from caterpillar through chrysalis to butterfly. It will teach you,
among other things, about the patience you need to develop to
allow growth to occur. The whole ritual process can be done right
in your kitchen. If you have a yard or access to a private natural
area, you may want to do the ceremony outdoors.

Planning: Now that you have clarified the intention, you can
assemble the symbolic Elements you will require. You can gather
seeds for sprouting, edible wild plants and flowers, if available,
salad ingredients, and a table for an altar. These all represent the
Element of Earth. For the Element of Air you will need a journal
for writing the thoughts and feelings that arise, and also some la-
bels for the jars. The Element of Water will be represented by the
water used for washing and soaking seeds, the quart jars for
sprouting, and a bowl for a salad. A large candle will represent
Fire and will be used in the invocation of the energy of spring.
Also a box of small candles (birthday candles would be appropriate) will be needed to connect with the inspiration and higher
guidance that Fire represents. Finally, Essence, the unifying Ele-

ment, will be represented by the sunlight, as well as by the tone that must constantly be present, almost as a mantra that says, "The outer reflects the inner world; the inner world resonates in harmony with the outer."

Emotional process: As we have said before, this is a process ritual, one of gradual awakening. Spending time with your thoughts and feelings each day will be part of the transformation facilitated by this ritual. The physical steps taken throughout the ritual can be thought of as mirrors, reflecting the feelings you are experiencing with your own cleansing and growth.

Physical preparation: These are the steps of the daily ritual: You are to choose one or more personal goals that you are working on "giving birth to," such as setting priorities, improving communication in a relationship, or getting into shape. Or you may choose something you are working on letting go of, for example, anxiety, depression, or procrastination. Match one of these with one of the types of seeds you have for sprouting. You might choose alfalfa seeds to denote procrastination and radish seeds to represent improving the way you would like to communicate in a relationship.

Make a label naming each of the goals you've developed. Put a handful of seeds in a quart jar with a screen or cheesecloth top. Label each jar with the goal that the seeds within represent. Pour enough water into each jar to cover the seeds, and leave them soaking overnight, imagining that as the seeds soak, so does the restrictive pattern of your "procrastination." For seeds to sprout, they must be rinsed and drained twice a day. It would be advantageous to save the waters you use for rinsing in a large container. Between rinsings, rest the jars on their sides on a kitchen counter. Each time you are ready to wash the seeds, you can first light one of the small candles. Use this as a point of focus, inspiration, and connection with your source of higher guidance. Meditate on your issues, and attend to any sense of limitation that comes up around them. You can use focusing questions such as, "What is my procrastination really about? How might procrastination be in some way a protection for me? What would my life be like if I did not avoid things I feel I should be doing?" Note in your journal both your thoughts and any feelings that arise during this process.

After a few days the seeds will crack and sprouts will emerge. Continue your process, matching your inner pace to the changes in the seeds and recording your experience in your journal. When the sprouts are about an inch long, and when you can get in touch with the sense of having grown in like manner, place the jar in the sun until the sprouts begin to green. The sun represents the energy of Essence. This symbolically calls for your growth to be recognized and nurtured by the Element of Essence as well.

Now your sprouts are ready for the culminating ceremony. This requires there be another *physical preparation.* For this part of the ritual, you will need your sprouts and other ingredients with which you can create a salad. If you live in or near a natural setting, you may want to take advantage of all the edible "weeds" that are so abundant in the spring, like miner's lettuce, chickweed, or dandelion greens. Symbolically, this is a way of saying that even what seem to be weeds—obstacles or useless materials—can really be nurturing and even medicinal! Also, many plants have edible flowers; nasturtiums are one of the most popular. Filling your salad with spring flowers is like filling your bowl with beauty and the life force that is manifested in the outer world in spring.

To create your altar, find a table you can bring to the ritual setting. A table can be transformed into an altar by first covering it with some special fabric, a table cloth, or a scarf. (See Chapter 8 for more information on erecting altars.) You can fill a vase with some spring flowers and place it on the altar. Find a large white candle and a holder for it. White candles are commonly used to represent the Element of Essence, as white is the blend of all colors. You can bring other items that symbolize spring for you, or any "power objects" you may have (Chapter 7 gives details on making ritual tools) to place on or around the altar, to help you to personalize the ritual. You will need the container of water you saved from rinsing the seeds, particularly if you will be doing the ritual outdoors. And of course, you will need your journal.

Before you begin the next part of the ritual, you will want to set aside an uninterrupted block of time to prepare, perform, and complete the process. As the ritual site will be transformed into a sacred space, it is essential that the site be a place you can feel assured will be private. Whatever you can do beforehand to bring forth that consecrated feeling is important. If you perform the ceremony in your kitchen, it would be helpful to clean and straighten it thoroughly. If you are outdoors, you may wish to somehow mark and clear a circle in which you can feel the energy to be different within than without. It is also crucial to prepare yourself. This is, after all, a celebration of personal transformation. Something in you is changing. You will want to bathe, perhaps with flowers, oils, or bubbles. Choose clothing that makes you feel special. You may want to decorate yourself in some way, possibly with face paint or with other ornamentation.

Manifestation: The enactment of the rite. *Creating a sacred space* can be the first ceremonial performed act. Consecrating and arranging your altar may be your first area of focus. After the altar has been arranged, some people like to cleanse and anoint their tools. Cleansing can be done energetically, with a sprinkling of salt or saltwater, with smudging (passing over burning herbs or incense, or any other way that suits you). Anointing can be done with scented waters or oils (see Chapter 7). You can also smudge or otherwise cleanse the ritual space. After everything within your circle is set, you can step outside of it. Stand at the edge or entrance to the space and take in the scene. Know that you are about to enter another world, a world that can be as magical as the world of your dreams and imagination. You can pass the burning incense around yourself, allowing the smoke to clear away any doubts or fears. Take three deep, full breaths. With each breath inhale a feeling of the extraordinary and exhale the ordinary. Step into the circle.

Declaration and enactment of intention: Kneel before your altar. Light and raise the candle. State that you are there to honor spring, birth, beginnings, growth, release, energy.

Invocation of larger energies: Ask that the essence of spring be there for you during the ritual. Ask that you may feel the qualities of spring alive within you to support and assist your own inner spring and sense of rebirth. Return the candle to the altar. You may want to put your hand on each of the items there to enhance your connection with what they represent. Sit with your journal and read through the notes from the past several days. Allow time to access and experience whatever feelings may be associated with your entries.

Take the ingredients for your salad. Meditate on what each of the items in your bowl means to you. Ask that your food be blessed and that it bring you strength to further your growth. Eat your salad, savoring the attention, care, and development it embodies.

When you are finished, pour the seed water into your bowl. Carry the water to a plant or place on the ground where you can pour it. As you give the water back to the Earth, let it be an offering to nourish the growth of other plants and a gift of gratitude to nature for its gifts.

Blessing and Closure: Return to the altar. Take the candle and walk clockwise around the circle or kitchen, thanking the essence of spring for attending your ritual, and allow this essence to withdraw. Placing the candle back on the altar, wet your fingers, and snuff the flame.

Grounding: The ceremony is complete.

Breakdown: You can carefully and thoughtfully return everything to its appropriate place or condition.

Evaluation: As you do this, consider what has occurred over the past several days. Are you satisfied with the process that has transpired? Is there anything that you would add or delete if you were to do it again? How do you think you may have benefited from this ritual?

Integration and actualization: In the following days, look for instances that show how your behavior has shifted. Notice if you seem to have more choices or a greater sense of freedom. Record your observations in your journal. Remind yourself of this ritual process whenever you are in a situation that involves your particular area of personal growth. Some of these changes may be subtle. Others may be noticeable only after a period of time has passed. Be gentle with yourself and grateful for what has occurred.

You may want to celebrate the arrival of spring with your friends. The following ritual is designed for a group of five to twenty people, and the ceremony itself will take approximately forty-five minutes. The plan is presented with you as the facilitator or coordinator, but you may want to work closely with a few of your friends or colleagues throughout the preparation stages, as well as during the ritual.

RITUAL FOR GROUP EXPRESSION

Preparation: In the individual ritual for spring, we discussed the emergence of life and new growth. It is the time of year when bulbs planted in the fall struggle through the earth to reach the air and light. Traditionally in Western religions it is a time of sacrifice and rebirth into a greater sense of freedom. At Passover, a lamb was sacrificed so that the firstborn sons could live. This led to the Exodus of the Jewish tribes to a new land as a free people. Christians celebrate Good Friday and Easter, when Jesus was crucified and resurrected. In this act the Christ offered freedom to the souls of humanity as well as the keys to "eternal life."

Clarifying the intention: Following this theme, the intention of this ritual is to honor the inspirations gestating within each of us; to recognize and release the aspects of ourselves that impede the birth of these inspirations; and to create ways to consciously help these inspirations to grow in ourselves and in the world.

Planning: Although we are presenting a complete ritual, you might want to take the time to allow your own unique creation to be expressed here. You can consider what kind of actions might represent gestation, struggle, sacrifice, and creation. How might the ritual space be arranged to represent these stages? Note your ideas and make a basic outline.

Each of the Elements needs to be represented in the ritual. While writing your plan you probably included some of them. Check and make sure all are present. As you do so, your plan will continue to develop. The following are the Elemental representations we selected for this ritual.

Earth ▽ The hibachi or brazier containing the central fire represents the winter earth holding the inspiration about to be born. You can use husks, shells, or some facsimile as a physical token of a protection no longer needed. To symbolize gestation, the room can be in darkness, with the group sitting or squatting within it. The sprouts that you and your friends have nurtured and brought represent the ways each of you has grown, and eating the salad signifies incorporating these qualities. Ask each person to bring a small gift that will exemplify what they feel is being born within them. The giving of the gift is a way to help that new quality find a place in the world.

Water ∇ Growth can be illustrated by movements, such as stretching or unfolding; or even more simply by something to drink. As we celebrate the increase of light, you may want to try orange juice with a little grenadine at the bottom—a sunrise.

Air △ When each member is ready to sacrifice a certain quality or way of being to the fire, he or she can state what that quality is, as a slip of paper naming the quality is put into the flames. After the sacrifice, the participants can create something by writing or drawing, or perhaps a group poem or story can be developed to express the release of inspiration.

Fire △ Inspiration is symbolized by the Element of Fire, and you can use a small central fire (in a brazier, hibachi, or some safe space outdoors; or simply an incense charcoal indoors) to represent this. This fire can be used to help "burn away" whatever the participants need to sacrifice to let their inspirations emerge.

Essence ⊙ The light from the central fire is the fount that draws and unites the participants in their darkness. After the sacrifice, the curtains can be drawn back or the lights turned on, as the participants come to the light of conscious awareness. Essence nourishes the soul as the sunlight has vitalized the seedlings. An invocation of Spirit at the beginning and a giving of thanks at the end of the ritual also acknowledge Essence. Another option is having the group clasp hands in a circle, the symbol for unity.

Now we can consider logistics, where you get down to details. The easiest way we know to cover all the bases is to use the journalist's formula of "who, what, when, where, and why."

Why has been covered in the section on clarifying your intention, so we can move on to the other categories.

Who is to be involved in the ritual? As you list the potential participants, consider if anyone would be offended by the ritual as it is planned. If children are to be involved, will the ritual be short enough to hold their attention and simple enough for them to understand?

During this phase of the planning you will need to delegate responsibilities. Who will gather what materials, set up, perform what stage of the ritual, do the cleanup, and so forth? Some of your friends may want to be involved in each of the stages of the ritual. As the Elements are represented in many ways throughout the process, assigning each individual to carry out the functions of a particular Element would be one way to allocate duties. This would give the person in charge of Fire, for example, the responsibility of bringing the charcoal, hibachi, and matches. They would set the fire up, light it and tend it, and take it down at the end. This is a practical way of sharing the work, as well as enlivening a particular quality in the person with each assignment.

Throughout the rest of this ritual plan, you as coordinator represent Essence. Choose one person to take on the duties of each of the other four Elements.

What needs to be done? What words need to be spoken? What order needs to be followed? Participants must be clear on how to prepare, what to bring, and what they are expected to do. Invitations need to be issued. The following list will give you an idea of how to determine which tasks can be performed by whom:

▽ Earth—bring food for a small salad, a salad bowl, and a tray; prepare a blessing for the salad.

▽ Water—bring orange juice, grenadine, clear plastic or glass cups; prepare a blessing to consecrate the drinks.

△ Air—make the invitations; bring light-colored construction paper, scissors, and a set of different colored felt-tip markers; prepare a blessing to affirm the creativity that is given its freedom during the ceremony.

△ Fire—bring a hibachi, a flat rock, a roll of incense charcoal, long matches, shaved cocoa shells, and a bowl to hold them; prepare a blessing for the fire.

☉ Essence—bring a white candle, candle holder and matches, spirits for the drinks (optional); prepare opening and closing remarks; prepare to lead the ritual; coordinate.

When includes not only the time the ritual is to be held but also the issuing of invitations, the gathering of ritual tools, and the time line of events within the ritual itself.

Where will the ritual be held? If it is to be outdoors, will there be enough privacy? Does the area you have chosen allow you the opportunity to feel a sense of containment? Is there enough room for what you have planned? Determine where within the ritual space participants will enter, stand, and move. Where will altars or objects be placed? You will find specific directions for this later in the section on Manifestation, the ritual itself.

After you've worked out the logistics and chosen the appropriate ritual Elements, it is time to go back to your basic idea and revamp it as needed. Plan out the ritual in sufficient detail, making notes about each step. As the coordinator, you need to know exactly what will happen during the ritual and be able to provide clear information to the other participants.

Emotional process: This is the time to check and see if you are remaining true to your intention and to note if you are feeling blocked in any way. More important, this is when you want to sit down and gently consider whatever feelings are present about what has been occurring. It is likely that there will be some emotional issues needing your attention. As you are in the position of Essence, you may find a resistance or hesitancy developing over the responsibilities of coordinating and helping the others stay in tune with the inspiration. Or you may find your ego becoming inflated with the power of your position. Whatever personal issues are being revealed, now is the time to work them through.

Other issues or emotional struggles can occur in the relationships of the participants. Are there any power struggles? Is anyone needing more say in the *what* and *how* of the ritual process? Does anyone feel nervous or insecure about their role? Working on these interpersonal issues with a compassionate, creative, problem-solving approach will make the preparations go more smoothly and add depth to the ritual itself.

Responsibility is always the child of consciousness. While clarifying your intention for this ritual, you considered how the ritual would affect people. Having come this far in your preparation, it is important to address this issue again. You have gotten in touch with your issues and those of your friends. As you reflect upon your intention and the ritual plan, can you discover if there may be any possibility for harm or exclusion that did not seem apparent before? If so, how can you best change this? As you grow on an ethical level, you replace walls with doors, each leading to opportunity.

Physical preparation: The first aspect of this step is an extension of what you covered in logistics. Well before the day of the ritual, invitations are issued, lists are made, and materials are collected. Everyone knows what they need to do and is prepared to do it. While this ritual may not require a rehearsal, other rituals do, and that would need to be orchestrated. When things have been satisfactorily coordinated, you can think about preparing yourself.

The individual ritual presented earlier is an excellent way to prepare for this group ritual. The outer self also needs preparation, and you may choose to fast or eat lightly the day of the ritual. Taking a bath in bubbles or oils and donning special clothing help create a kind of purification. You might also want to meditate on the intention, ask for higher guidance, and go over the ritual one more time before the others arrive.

Before you bathe and dress, the ritual space needs to be made ready. Move the furniture as needed, dust, vacuum, and clean the space. For this ritual, where Essence symbolically enters the gathering as light shining in through the windows, make sure that the windows are clean and that the curtains or shades open easily. After you have completed the cleansing in the room and of yourself, you can return to the room to clear the space energetically. A simple way to do this is to stand in the center of the area, facing east, and light a candle to ask Spirit to help in clearing out all that does not harmonize with the purpose of the ceremony. Then starting from the east walking clockwise around the room, stop at each quadrant, asking for clarity of thought in the east, proper direction of energy from the south, emotional depth and compassion from the west, and groundedness and proper action from the north. Return to the east to complete the circle, then move to the center to thank Spirit for help in clearing the circle. Leave the area quietly.

Once your friends arrive with the items for the ritual, you can begin to set up. Water prepares a tray of sunrise drinks in the kitchen, and Earth creates a small salad. Air cuts egg shapes out of the construction paper. Fire puts the shaved cocoa shells into a bowl. You draw the curtains and set a fire extinguisher outside of the circle but close at hand. When everything is ready, you and Fire enter the ritual space respectfully. You help her set up the hibachi on a flat stone in the center of the circle, and she places the incense charcoal into it that she will later light. Each person in turn sets up the symbols of their Elements and quietly stands before them. You say a short blessing and thank the group for their work. All quietly leave the circle.

Manifestation: Once the space has been set up and the other guests have arrived, you can guide them into the ritual circle around the hibachi. You and Water are in the west, in front of the sunrises. Earth is in the north, standing before the salad. Air stands in the east, pens and paper ready, and Fire in the south with the bowl of cocoa shells. The other guests fill in the circle.

To begin you might say, "Welcome! Before we start, let's be silent for a moment, take a few deep breaths, and let go of any outer distractions we are holding. Allow yourself to feel the fondness we all have for each other and the caring and love that is present in this place today. We ask that the larger love as represented by the unity of Essence also be present here, and that what we do today be guided by that force, that we may help ourselves and the world to be touched with love and light."

Declaration of intention: You may wish to talk about the feelings of coming through the winter months and beginning to experience the life associated with spring rising in us again. This dialogue can lead into the statement of intention: "We ask that this ritual honor the inspirations gestating within us; that we may recognize and release that which impedes the birth of these inspirations within us; and that we are able to create ways for these inspirations to come to consciousness in ourselves and in the world." Clearly explain the phases of this ceremony, and ask the participants to sit or squat as a way of representing the dormancy of winter.

Invocation of larger energies: Now Fire lights the central fire and speaks of the inner light kindled at the winter solstice, which has been gestating since then and is approaching the time of birth. Ask the participants to focus within on the power of this growth and to imagine trying to rise but being unable to do so. "What gets in your way? Seeds have to break through their shells to grow; what is *your* shell? What part of you, what quality, stops your growth right now? Allow a word, phrase, or image to come forth identifying this quality. Let yourself feel the limitations it imposes on you and also what your life could be like without it. Imagine how, free of this limitation, your inner spark would grow in the spring, take form during the summer, and come to full manifestation in the fall."

As you speak, Earth moves clockwise around the circle, giving each participant some cocoa shells. You instruct each person to come to the central fire as they are ready, and speak the word that represents their limitation or shell over the cocoa shells, which they then sacrifice to the fire. When all members have come forward and symbolically released that which has hindered their growth, Fire can ask that Spirit accept these surrenderings, and that the participants accept the truth that some quality that may have been an important part of their behavior can change.

As the sweet smoke of the burning shells rises upward, you can direct everyone to focus within and discover their feelings of constriction lifting and dispersing. Then, while all slowly rise, you can draw back the curtains, invoking the light and love and power of Essence to assist in recognition and acceptance of growth.

Everyone will stretch a bit, glad of the light and freedom. At this time, Air can walk clockwise around the circle, giving out pens and paper eggs. You explain that the eggs represent that which has been liberated. On their egg, each person is to draw symbols, pictures, or write whatever they feel expresses this freedom. Now Earth goes around the circle again, this time holding a tray with the salad bowl. As each person places the sprouts they grew in the past week into the bowl, they also put their egg on the tray, speaking briefly of their release.

Earth then raises the bowl up and asks a blessing of Essence for the salad, to incorporate not only the inspirations just born but the presence and constancy of Spirit. The salad is offered to the group and all partake of it.

Water then goes around the circle distributing the sunrise drinks. Everyone holds up the cup for a blessing as Water speaks of what is being symbolized. The blessing is made and everyone drinks. Next Air asks for a blessing for the paper eggs, that the experience they represent will be remembered. Each person then reclaims their egg.

You explain that the gifts represent what each person felt was to be born and they can now be passed on. As you give yours to the person on your left, you speak briefly about the significance of your gift and, if you wish, how it relates to your experience in this ritual. This process continues around the circle until the person on your right has spoken and passed their gift to you.

Giving thanks, blessing, and closure: After the cups have been collected and set aside, all hold hands in a circle. Ask that everyone give thanks to themselves, to each other, and to Essence for the experience, the growth, and the togetherness. You can also ask Spirit to help you bring the energy and consciousness gained during the rite into the world.

Grounding: The ritual is over, but before you and your friends begin to socialize, there are a few things that need to be done. If there is any food left over that has been blessed, it should be consumed before the circle is closed. Or it can be saved and buried. Any leftover drinks can be poured on the ground as a libation. The blessings have made the food sacred, and it deserves respect.

To release the circle, you might stand in the center and say, "We thank thee, Spirit, for your presence here today. The work is done, and we release this sacred space to normal space," and clap your hands loudly. Extinguish the candle you lit when clearing the space. You can then break down the ritual set up, each person being in charge of their Element.

The circle breaks, people take their gifts and exit the space, going to another room to dance, talk, and celebrate the arrival of spring.

Emotional Process: During the party note how you feel. You might find greater expression in your dancing or a fuller love for your friends. People will probably thank you for the ritual. It is likely that you will feel elation at a large project being successfully completed, and it is important to remember that, while you coordinated the ritual, it was the access to experiencing Essence that permitted growth, change, and connection.

Evaluation: Use the feedback from the people at the party, and discussion with the core group, to help you evaluate what worked well, what could have been done better, and how. Assess your work as coordinator and the effectiveness of the ritual as a whole. Add notes to the end of your ritual plan, so that if you perform this ritual again, you can improve it.

Integration and Actualization: Over the next week or so, be aware of how you access the inner change that occurred for you during the ritual. How do you bring it into the world? Look for opportunities to change old behavior patterns, and keep track in your journal of your emotional responses to these changes. There may be times when you feel unable to change, to let go of the limitation of, for example, unreasonable fear, as you were able to do during the ritual. Remember that ritual is a powerful tool in creating change, but that change is still a gradual process, which takes time, energy, and courage. Call on Spirit and the power of the ritual experience to help you. When you receive help, give thanks.

Another way to help actualize the sense of inner release experienced in the ritual is to meet with your four friends to discuss how you are all faring during this part of the process. As the group that created the ritual together, you have greater access to the energy of the ceremony than you have individually. Together you can brainstorm ideas for implementing change in your lives and give each other perspective and support for your individual work. The group can also celebrate the steps toward growth taken by each of you. The unity and increased closeness of the group can be a reminder of your successful connection with Essence.

Chapter 12

Conclusion

It is the nature of human beings to grow, to evolve, to increase relationships with ourselves, each other, our world, and with our sense of Spirit. The substance of our lives is based in this process. Connecting with our creative resources, our recognition of wholeness, and more important, with the knowledge that we are part of something much larger that is eternal and omnipresent, is what makes the difference between merely existing and living fully.

For most of our history as a species, ritual has been a viable access to such a connection. The rituals our ancestors used thousands of years ago afforded these connections as early human life centered around surviving in a difficult environment. Rituals focused on the land, the seasons, the hunt, and relationships within the tribe or between tribes. For our more recent ancestors, and particularly for us, surviving in the environment is much more complicated. The rituals that have been handed down to us are frequently insufficient to address and satisfy our personal and spiritual needs and are often unable to heal us from separation and alienation. It is more than apparent that our society and our world are in a frightening and dangerous condition.

The two of us have been practicing the symbolic and ritual arts for twenty years and working as counselors and teachers for over a decade. It is through our own inner quests and our intimate work with people experiencing pain, confusion, and hopelessness that we have come to recognize the need for personalized and meaningful rituals in people's lives. As necessity is said to be the mother of invention, we found ourselves creating and performing rituals for ourselves, our friends and families, our clients and students. To do so we have had to be aware of the people with whom we are working as they stand before us and of

"In order to arrive there, To arrive where you are, to get from where you are not, You must go by a way wherein there is no ecstasy.
In order to arrive at what you do not know You must go by a way which is the way of ignorance. In order to possess what you do not possess You must go by the way of dispossession. In order to arrive at what you are not You must go through the way in which you are not.
And what you do not know is the only thing you know And what you own is what you do not own And where you are is where you are not."
—T.S. Eliot
Four Quartets

how religious, cultural, racial, socioeconomic, and historical influences have affected who they are and who they are becoming.

This expanded perception has been combined with our personal explorations of myth, cross-cultural and spiritual practices, mysticism, and the arts. From this panoply of resources, we've developed and refined the ritual process presented in this book. In a reciprocal manner, using the ritual process can open you to a new experience of wholism, as you draw from the wealth of the peoples of this planet.

This book has presented you with the facets and process common to rituals, different types of rituals, and examples of ways to apply them. By now your awareness and understanding is likely to have shifted, even if you have not yet begun to practice the art of ritual. Here is a recap of some of the primary ideas you have been reading about. You may be surprised at how much seems familiar.

ELEMENTAL CORRESPONDENCES

By now you are probably feeling comfortable with the concept of the four Elements—Fire, Air, Water and Earth—and perhaps you are beginning to relate these Elements to different parts of your daily life. By doing so you can increase the sense of the sacred in yourself and your world. To help you in that endeavor, here is a chart of some possible correspondences to the Elements, including how the Elements relate to different kinds of rituals, the ritual process, and applications.

ELEMENT	FIRE △	AIR △	WATER ▽	EARTH ▽
SYMBOL	Flames	Bell, Incense	Cup	Disc, Cube
COLOR	Red	Blue	Silver	Earth Tones
GEOMETRY	Point	Line	Plane	Solid
STATE OF MATTER	Combustion	Gas	Liquid	Solid
PERSONAL FACET	Energy	Mind	Feeling	Body
ASPECT OF RELATIONSHIPS	Passion	Communication	Emotion	Affection
LEARNING	Desire	Study	Integration	Application
CREATIVITY	Inspiration	Planning	Process	Product
RITUALS				
TYPE	Beginning	Merging	Cycle	Ending
WORLD	Inspiration Energy	Creation Mental	Deepening Feeling	Manifestation Action
APPLICATION	Individual	Relationships	Family	Group

THE PROCESS OF RITUAL

PREPARATION	△ Fire: Intention
	△ Air: Planning
	▽ Water: Emotional Process
	▽ Earth: Physical Preparation
MANIFESTATION	▽ Earth: Creating a Sacred Space
	▽ Water: Setting the Mood
	△ Air: Declaring the Intention
	△ Fire: Invocation
	△ Air: Direction of Higher Energies
	▽ Water: Blessing
	▽ Earth: Closure
GROUNDING	▽ Earth: Breakdown of Sacred Space
	▽ Water: Emotional Process
	△ Air: Evaluation
	△ Fire: Integration

In a ritual, each object, action, or word has mythic significance. We have found that ritual reminds us that in normal life this is also true—a concept we tend to forget when we get caught up in the compelling lure of form and accomplishment. The hunger for value so prevalent in our society illuminates the need to recognize the power in conscious awareness, in purposeful action. Life is not meaningless unless we do not attend to the meaning inherent in existence. The sacred is always present, always available. We need only remember to step back from the bustle and drudgery of daily life to receive it.

Ritual is a tool to focus our attention on meaning; this is a skill we can develop to enhance each moment of our lives. To be truly present in our own lives is an ability we must develop if we are to continue building a foundation of relatedness and beauty in a world that can seem so divided and in pain. The new paradigm of wholism has been embraced increasingly over the last twenty years and is being felt on all levels of reality. This book is a manifestation of that growth, and we hope it has served the purpose of allowing more light, joy, meaning, and sacredness into your life.

Glossary

Air △ one of the Elements; a symbolic representation of the mind and thought, ideas, distinction, and understanding

altar a table or platform, usually raised, used in a sacred ceremony to hold offerings, power objects, or ritual items

archetype from Jungian psychology—an innate energy pattern of the psyche that will be expressed symbolically

collective unconscious from Jungian psychology—the deepest layers of the unconscious, where memories and potentialities exist on a universal level and are available to everyone

Earth ▽ one of the Elements; a symbolic representation of that which is solid, tangible, has a sense of history, provides support and practicality

Element the archetypal substances that are the basic component parts or principles of any thing

Essence ☉ the underlying and unifying nature of any thing; used as the fifth Element, and bringing a sense of wholeness

fetish something specially crafted to serve as a power object

Fire △ one of the Elements; it symbolically represents passion, force, courage, vitality, and revolution or possibility

mythology the stories or legends of a people; the beliefs by which we live

numerology a numerical system used to help understand life; often applied to understanding personality characteristics

Ouroborous the snake biting its own tail; the Great Round, the eternal cyclicity

psyche an autonomous factor; the source of all human activities, being at once the conscious mind, the personal unconscious, and the collective unconscious

ritual a ceremony, particularly formalized, used to fulfill a certain intention

shamanism a spiritual practice that brings wisdom, healing, and change, based on the belief in the unity of all things and the honoring of all that is

skrying gazing into a reflective object to achieve insight or illumination

Spirit life force energy; the divine force

Tarot a set of seventy eight cards, used primarily for self-understanding, and also for understanding the larger relationships among self and others, others, and things as a whole

transpersonal beyond the persona or mask; energy or awareness that transcends the personal

Water ∇ one of the Elements; representative of feelings, sensitivity, inner process

Wicca the old religion, the religion of the Great Goddess, a nature religion that honored the harmony and unity of all things

Bibliographic References

Z'ev ben Shimon Halevi, *School of Kabbalah* (York Beach, ME: 1985).

N. Fredman and R. Sherwood, *Handbook of Structured Techniques in Marriage and Family Therapy* (New York: Brunner/Mazel, Inc., 1986).

Marion Woodman, *Addiction to Perfection* (Toronto: Inner City Books, 1982).

Starhawk, *Dreaming the Dark* (Boston: Beacon Press, 1982).

Edward Whitmont, *Return of the Goddess* (New York: Crossroad Publishing Company, 1984).

Fritz Perls, *The Gestalt Approach and Eye Witness to Therapy* (Ben Lomond, CA: Science and Behavior Books, 1973).

Onno van der Hart, *Rituals in Psychotherapy* (New York: Irvington Publishers, 1983).

John A. Sanford, *Healing and Wholeness* (New York: Paulist Press, 1977).

J. E. Cirlot, *A Dictionary of Symbols* (New York: Philosophical Library, Inc., 1962).

Charles Ponce, *Kabbalah* (London: Quest Books, 1973).

Joseph Campbell, *Myths to Live By* (New York: Bantam Books, 1972).

Richard Wilhelm, *I Ching* (New Jersey: Princeton University Press, 1967).

C. G. Jung, *Analytical Psychology Its Theory and Practice,* (New York: Random House, 1968).

Starhawk, *The Spiral Dance* (San Francisco: Harper and Row Publishers, 1979).

Joseph Campbell, *The Power of Myth* (New York: Doubleday, 1988).

André Malraux, *Les Métamorphoses des dieux* (1957) in *The International Thesaurus of Quotations* (New York: Harper and Row, 1970).

Mircea Eliade, *Myths, Dreams, and Mysteries* (New York: Harper and Row, 1957).

William G. Gray, *Ladder of Lights* (London: Helios Books, 1968).

T. S. Eliot, *Four Quartets* (New York: Harcourt, Brace and World, 1971).